# Still Room for Hope

# Still Room for Hope

## A Survivor's Story of Sexual Assault, Forgiveness, and Freedom

## Alisa Kaplan

New York Boston Nashville

FaithWords
Hachette Book Group
1290 Avenue of the Americas
New York, NY 10104

www.faithwords.com

Printed in the United States of America

RRD-C

First edition: April 2015

10 9 8 7 6 5 4 3 2 1

FaithWords is a division of Hachette Book Group, Inc.
The FaithWords name and logo are trademarks of Hachette Book Group, Inc.

The Hachette Speakers Bureau provides a wide range of authors for speaking events. To find out more, go to www.hachettespeakersbureau.com or call (866) 376-6591.

The publisher is not responsible for websites (or their content) that are not owned by the publisher.

Library of Congress Cataloging-in-Publication Data has been applied for.

ISBN 978-1-4555-5383-9

*This book is dedicated to every survivor of sexual assault and anyone who has ever gone to the depths of hell and thought you would never find your way back.*

*There is a beautiful life waiting for you to grasp it with both hands. Don't ever give up!*

# Contents

# CONTENTS

# Author's Note

This is my story. I have told it using court documents, media reports, my family's records, and my own memories and journals. Any inaccuracies are unintentional.

Because of the nature of the story, and to protect the privacy of others, I have changed some of the names and identifying details.

Some readers may find the graphic nature of the material disturbing, and survivors of sexual assault or abuse may find some scenes emotionally triggering. Please take care of yourself.

*There is no easy walk to freedom anywhere, and many of us will have to pass through the valley of the shadow of death again and again before we reach the mountaintop of our desires.*

—Nelson Mandela

# Introduction

*August 20, 2005*
*San Bernardino County, Southern California*

"One week, you hear me? Seven days."

The cop's experienced, weary glance took in everything about me: the sunken eyes surrounded by bruise-colored flesh, the filthy T-shirt hanging off my emaciated frame, the infected scabs marring my face, bare arms, and legs.

Still, he was giving me a second chance.

I was nineteen years old and addicted to methamphetamine. My desperate parents had kicked me out of my childhood home, and I was staying with my abusive boyfriend, Russell, in a one-bedroom drug house with ten other people, including three young kids. The cops had come to arrest Russell on an outstanding warrant for stealing cars, and since I was clearly under the influence in a house full of drugs, they were going to take me in, too. But then the cop rifling through my purse found something that gave him pause: a list of the overcrowded drug rehab centers I'd been calling for weeks, begging for a bed.

At the time, I was still a Jane Doe, the anonymous victim at the center of one of the most notorious rape cases in California history—the event that had sent my life off the rails. But just as that cop had no idea of the trauma that had brought me to that meth house (or any inkling that I was the girl he'd heard about everywhere, from CNN to 20/20 to the pages of LA Weekly), neither would he recognize me today: a healthy, powerful woman, joyful in my recovery and confident in God's love.

That police raid was one of the first moments where I saw a glimmer of hope for my own future, so that is where I chose to begin this story. It was a lesson for me that even in the very darkest moments of our lives, there is always—always—room for hope.

A meth house isn't where you'd expect to find a former straight-A student, color guard captain, and cross-country star from a solid, loving, intact family. It wasn't where I expected to find myself, either. But in July 2002, when I was sixteen years old, my life turned upside down.

One night that summer, I was raped. I use the word *rape*, although my assailants were not convicted of rape; they were convicted of other sexual assault charges. Still, from an emotional and spiritual perspective, rape remains my experience of what occurred, despite what the jury said. And since this book is an account of how I experienced it, rape is what I will be calling what happened that night. Despite video evidence of the assault, the first trial—an experience that was more traumatic for me than the attack was—ended in a hung jury. I fared better during the second trial, but the four years it took to convict my assailants took a terrible toll on me. By the time the trials were over, I was addicted to meth, alienated from my close-knit family, and living on the streets.

Thankfully, my story doesn't end there.

In the twelve years that have passed since then, I have gotten clean. I have found the work I am supposed to be doing, work that draws on my own experiences to help other victims become survivors. I have found my faith again, faith that is stronger from my journey through the valley of the shadow of darkness. And I learned to forgive not just my friends who abandoned me, the attorneys who defamed me, and those in the media who publicly humiliated me, but also my assailants—and myself.

Although I would never have asked for what happened to me, I cannot deny that in the long, slow process of recovering, I have become the woman I was meant to be.

I'd never thought about writing a book until I started speaking to other survivors. Unfortunately, there are a lot of us. One in every six women in America will experience sexual assault in their lifetimes. It is estimated that a woman is raped every two minutes in this country—and yet, it is still deeply taboo for us to talk about it. Since I have started telling my story, many women have told me that I have inspired them to speak out, too, to tell their families or partners about what happened to them. More than one woman has told me that my story gave her the courage to finally report her assault, many years afterward.

But I quickly learned that victims of sexual assault weren't the only survivors seeking me out. In fact, many of the people who had the strongest reactions to my story weren't victims of violence at all. Instead, they were people who'd lost loved ones to a prolonged cancer battle, people who'd gone through difficult divorces, people who'd lost their homes because of financial misfortune or a natural disaster—all kinds of people living through things they didn't think they could survive.

The specifics of their stories might have been different from mine, but they were all trauma survivors, and they were looking to me as someone who had made it to the other side for the inspiration they needed to get there themselves.

Every one of us will, at some point in our lives, face a challenge that tests us at our very core. All of us will find ourselves at a point where we simply don't know if we have the strength to go on. Every one of us needs to know how it will feel to put down the burden of guilt and shame, and to begin to take steps toward forgiving the unforgivable. No matter what we're going through, we need to know that there is an "after"—that it will, with time, be possible to trust again, to experience hope and happiness.

My intention with this book is to bring hope to everyone who has been to the depths of hell and felt, even for a moment, that they can't find their way back. Because I know that with a little help, we can all rise and answer whatever challenges life delivers us.

No matter what has happened to you, you are not alone. There is a joyful, glorious, meaningful life out there, one that is filled with light and laughter and love, waiting for you to be ready for it.

This is the path I have walked, and it is the story that I want to tell.

# CHAPTER ONE

## *They Wouldn't Do That to You*

Around ten a.m. on July 6, 2002, I woke up in the passenger seat of my own stinking hot car, sick as a dog, disoriented, and covered in vomit. The interior of the car was so hot that I could barely breathe. It felt like I was inhaling fire.

A woman was knocking on the passenger-side window. I had never met her before, but I knew who she was: my boyfriend Brian's mother. I looked around. I was parked around the corner from Brian's house. He must have driven my car to his neighborhood before leaving for work. I could remember nothing about how I'd gotten there or the night before.

The woman outside knocked again and gestured for me to come out. I stumbled out of the car and followed her into their house. Brian had told her I was sleeping off a hangover, she told me, but she'd grown concerned when the day started getting hot and she saw that the windows of the car were rolled up.

I was startled by a glimpse of my reflection in a window. Vomit matted my long blond hair, and my face was puffy and blotchy, as if I were still drunk. I looked really rough. Now I could see why she looked so concerned. But I was preoccupied by the big blank hole where my own memories of the night before should have been. I had gone to my friend Seth's beach house to hang out with him and to see Brian. Another guy, Jared, had been there, too. Why couldn't I remember anything else?

"You drank way too much last night," Brian's mom told me, handing me a glass of water.

"I don't know," I said, confused, but trying not to be rude. "I only had a little bit of a drink that Jared made me."

"Did you smoke weed?" she asked me.

I told her I had, but only a single hit.

She nodded, satisfied. "That's what happened. The combination of the alcohol and weed knocked you out."

I agreed with her to be polite, but I could barely form words and getting the glass of water to my mouth was almost more than I could manage. That little bit of booze and weed should not have messed me up as badly as I was messed up that morning.

Brian's mother made me a piece of toast, to "soak up the alcohol," and told me again that the combination of the drinking and the drugs had done me in. "You just need to sleep it off," she said again. I didn't know her well enough to argue, and I was feeling scarily tired and unwell. After another awkward minute, I decided to drive to my best friend's house so I could get cleaned up before going home.

Adriana and I were inseparable that year. We'd been introduced by my friend Melaney, someone I'd known since junior high. Melaney and I had gone to different high schools, but we'd started hanging out again only a few months earlier. Melaney's friends from her new school were different from the athletic, academic-minded kids we'd been friends with before. These kids were richer, better looking. Their houses were bigger, and there was much less adult supervision. They drank and smoked pot. One of them was Adriana, and it was through her that I'd met Brian and Seth.

I have no memory of the drive over to her house. When I think about it now, I realize that it's a miracle I made it there in one piece. I couldn't get my bearings. What was wrong with me? Even if I'd gotten completely wasted the night before, it was almost noon; I couldn't still be drunk. On my way there, I called my mom and told her my girlfriends and I were on our way to Six Flags. As I talked to her, I could hear myself slurring my words. I wasn't drunk, but my brain was acting like I was.

By the time I got to Adriana's house, a golf ball–sized lump on my head throbbed painfully. I headed straight for the bathroom. When I pulled down my jeans to pee, my bra fell out. Urinating was so painful and bloody that I called for Adriana from the toilet. I was afraid to wipe myself.

But it was only when I pulled off my shirt to get into the shower and saw the bruises emerging on my neck, shoulders, and back reflected in the mirror that I first thought the word *rape*.

"I can't remember anything about last night," I told

3

Adriana. "I'm pretty sure I had sex with someone without knowing it." She was having none of it. "You were just really drunk," she said. People kept saying that—but I knew I'd had only one beer and a single hit of pot before Jared gave me a drink that tasted like pine needles, the last thing I could remember.

"No," I insisted. "I think something happened."

These were boys we knew, boys we trusted. "They wouldn't do that to you," she insisted.

I wanted to believe her. But I couldn't escape the growing apprehension that there might have been something in the drink Jared had made for me.

After I got out of the shower, Adriana came in to the bathroom, holding my ringing cell phone. I was shocked to see that the call was from Jared. I took the phone—and here's what I eventually testified to the jury about what happened next.

"How you feeling?"

"Jared, what happened last night? I can't remember anything, and I'm really messed up."

"Why? You sore?" he said, laughing.

His tone sounded light and mocking to me, as if we were sharing a joke, and I felt suddenly sure that whatever had happened at that beach house the night before had been very serious—and very bad.


Growing up, I'd been the good girl with the good grades.

More than anything, I wanted to move to New York to

be a journalist. Justin Timberlake aside, I wasn't all that focused on boys, or even on the ultimate dream of having a family. My fantasies about my future all focused on being successful and respected, a fearless journalist who championed the underdog and shed light on little-understood issues, someone who changed the world.

I was born seven weeks premature, so tiny and sick that the doctors told my parents to say goodbye. But when my father reached into the incubator to touch my hand for the last time, I grabbed onto his finger so hard he thought I'd break it. "I don't think this little girl is going anywhere just yet," he told my mom. "She's a fighter."

As a little kid, I had always loved to participate—and to win. In fifth grade, I iced my forehead and tricked my mom into letting me go to school with a fever of 103, because I didn't want to mess up my perfect attendance record. I loved being a Girl Scout and relished the sense of achievement I got from seeing my sash fill with badges, representing all that I'd accomplished and learned, all the challenges I'd met and beaten.

Being a Girl Scout also gave me the opportunity to serve. I volunteered at convalescent homes, cleaned up the local parks, and served as a big sister for the younger scouts, helping to plan their ceremonies and camping trips. I loved feeling useful and helpful.

In junior high school, I got very involved with yearbook, and I spent a couple of weeks every summer refining my skills at yearbook camp. I loved it. Not only were my yearbook responsibilities deadline-oriented, but they allowed me to stretch myself. I loved organizing all the photos and text, writing funny captions, and meticulously laying out each of the pages. My friends Hanna and Melaney and I would stay up all night making sure each layout was perfect. Picture the Three Musketeers, only nerdy.

I was also an athlete. In junior high, I joined the color guard and the dance team. I'm a perfectionist and a natural competitor, a trait my teammates loved until the day I was chosen to be captain of the color guard, and then the eye-rolling started: I wouldn't give them a moment's rest until they had the routine nailed. In my freshman year of high school, I was on the volleyball and track teams. My sophomore year, I made junior varsity cross-country, which meant training up to ten miles a day.

I loved running. I loved the feeling of running, my mind empty except for the Southern California scenery, my limbs working in perfect synchronicity. Many mornings, my dad would ride his bike alongside me during my long training runs, telling me jokes to keep me going. He and my mom never missed a single one of my races. They'd stand on the sidelines hollering their love and encouragement, often taking a shortcut through the course so they could cheer for me and my friends from multiple spots. When they took me out for burgers and fries afterward, I basked in their support and in their loving pride.

In addition to all of my extracurriculars, I excelled at school. If there was a bonus problem on a test, I did it. If there was an essay I could write for extra credit, I wrote it. When I was ten, my dad told me he'd buy me the car of my dreams for my sixteenth birthday if I got straight A's all the way through elementary and middle and high school. He figured it was a bet he'd never have to pay, but he didn't factor my stubbornness into the equation—a little surprising, considering that he's the one I got it from. But, like me, he's a man of his word, and on my sixteenth birthday, after six years of great grades my parents sent me on a scavenger hunt that ended behind the wheel of a cobalt-blue Mustang convertible.

That car was a game changer. Not only was I the only one of my friends with a car, but it was a really awesome car. And it wasn't only my old friends from color guard and Girl Scouts who wanted rides, but the popular kids that Adriana and Melaney were starting to spend their weekends with. They were richer, better dressed, and better looking, but my Mustang was cool enough to catch their attention.

This was a big deal to me. I'd always had a lot of friends. I liked to know everybody. I didn't hang out exclusively with the kids from yearbook or the volleyball team. Instead, I'd walk through the lunchroom, stopping for a chat with a buddy at every single table.

But having a lot of friends didn't exactly mean that I was popular. Everybody may have liked me, but being in charge of the yearbook doesn't make you Queen Bee. In elementary school, I'd worn glasses, and I'd been a little chubby. I spent most of my time trailing after my older brother and his friends, so you'd probably have called my wardrobe tomboyish, if you were being charitable. (I

favored long, baggy T-shirts with cute sayings on them.)
All of this meant that while I had lots of friends who were
boys, they weren't exactly knocking down the door to date
me—not that my parents would have agreed to let me date
before I was sixteen.

By junior high, the fashion sense I inherited from my
mom, the ultimate girly girl, had started to kick in. (You'll
never see my mom in sloppy sweats and flip-flops. She'll
put a cute top and little heels on, even if she's just running
out to get a quart of milk.) Suddenly I wasn't leaving the
house unless I was wearing a coordinated outfit and had my
mascara and lip gloss on.

By the time I got to high school, the seven to ten miles I
ran every day to train for cross-country and track had taken
care of whatever extra puppy fat I was carrying. And I had
that cobalt Mustang. It didn't take long before I was finding myself invited to parties, the kind where there were no
parents but lots of booze. The kinds of boys I had never
dreamed would ever pay attention to me were showing off
in front of me, teasing me, flirting, asking for my number.

The kids who hung out on Prep Hill were at the absolute top of the pecking order. And they wanted me.

I was completely besotted with my newfound social status and prepared to do anything I had to in order to fit in. I
craved attention, and, like many sixteen-year-olds, I wasn't
particularly good at differentiating between the good and
the bad kinds of attention. Because I'd spent so much time
wrapped up in geeky pursuits like yearbook, I was probably a little naïve, too.

It was precisely because I'd always been such a good kid that my parents felt okay about giving me a lot of freedom. I'd never gotten into serious trouble. The worst thing I'd ever tried to do was to sneak backstage at an NSYNC concert. By nature, my parents are careful, even to the point of being a little overprotective, and they checked up on me regularly. But until that summer between sophomore and junior years, I was always where I'd told them I'd be— usually practicing dance moves with my friends in their bedrooms, hanging out and listening to music in our backyard, or watching movies in the den. So they had no reason not to trust me.

Their own history had quite a bit to do with it, too. My dad had been popular in high school. He'd done his share of partying, and he knew how compelling it could be to hang out with the cool kids. My mom, on the other hand, had been a complete nerd, right up until her senior year. She didn't drink, and she'd never done an illegal drug in her life. She'd gone from ugly duckling to swan in her senior year, but in her heart she still had the practical, sensible attitude of that ugly duckling. So she was completely unprepared for the transformation I went through.

What surprises me now is how quickly my life changed sophomore year. I got the Mustang in January. At the time, I didn't drink, but that soon changed. I didn't smoke pot, either, until the most gorgeous guy I'd ever seen in my life passed me a joint. At the very first unchaperoned house party I attended, two things happened: I got drunk for the first time, and I lost my virginity. I was growing up on overdrive, and I quickly gained a reputation as a party girl.

During the spring of my sophomore year, I met a cocky, wealthy skateboarder called Seth, who introduced me to his friend Brian. Brian was great-looking and known for his gentleness and for being a good guy. I was smitten. We started seeing each other more often, and Brian became my first real boyfriend.

That summer, our family received a terrible shock. My beloved grandpa died, suddenly and without warning. We were in the car on our way to see him when we got the call. He was scheduled to leave that morning for a house he'd bought in Oregon, where he could relax and fish his days away, and we were headed over to send him off with a big celebratory brunch. Then my dad's cell phone rang: "He's not moving." In the time it took us to finish the drive to their house, it was official. My grandpa was dead.

I took it hard. The two of us had always been deeply connected. He had loved to announce loudly in public that I was his favorite granddaughter. Then he'd throw me a wink: We both knew that I was the only female grandkid. Now, Phil Kaplan was not an easy man. He'd grown up in Brooklyn, the son of Austrian Jews who had fled to North America, so poor that when he was a baby, he slept in a dresser drawer. He'd worked hard to pull himself out of poverty and to make a life for himself, and you don't do that without being smart and tough. So my grandpa didn't have a lot of patience for weakness or stupidity, or a lot of tact when he was confronting it, but he had a giant soft spot for one person, and that was me. The night he died, I went out with my friends and got drunk.

Two weeks after his death, it was the Fourth of July. A group of my best girlfriends and I went out to Seth's dad's beach house. It was the craziest party I'd ever been to, with lots of pot and alcohol. Brian was there, and he introduced me to a new guy, Jared, a friend of Seth's. I disliked him immediately. When he looked at me, the hackles rose on the back of my neck.

The next night, Seth, Brian, and Jared invited me and my girlfriends to come back to the beach house for another party. At first I said no, because Adriana had been grounded and couldn't go. I didn't want to stay home, but I'd already told my parents I was staying at Adriana's, and her mom wouldn't let me sleep over. I had nowhere else to go.

Right from the beginning, I had a bad feeling about heading out there. After I'd said I'd go, I got so sick to my stomach that I threw up at work. (I now believe this was God warning me not to go.) But, despite my misgivings, I decided to drive out to the beach house by myself.

It would prove to be the worst decision I'd ever made.

I want to be very clear here: There's absolutely no excuse for sexual misconduct. If I have my way, everyone who reads this book will have a conversation with the young men in their lives to help them to understand the clear boundaries between right and wrong, the power of the bystander, and the importance of clear, sober, enthusiastic consent before any sexual contact takes place.

That's what I'd encourage you to tell your sons, and it's what I'll tell mine, if I ever have them.

That's what I'll tell my daughters, too, if I ever have them. But I won't stop there.

In an ideal world, nobody would have to guarantee our safety, but we don't live in an ideal world. In fact, sexual assault and abuse happen all the time. Every year in America, there are more than two hundred thousand sexual assaults, which translates roughly to one every two minutes. Of those, 44 percent of victims are—as I was—under the age of eighteen. And these numbers are highly conservative. According to a 2013 report by the National Research Council, there is increasing reason to suspect that cases of rape and sexual assault are dramatically undercounted.

The only way we will stop rape is if men stop raping. But I believe there are things that women can do to minimize the risks we take. I only wish I'd realized that at sixteen. I should not have gone out to that beach house by myself. Period, end of story. Should I have been able to without worrying that I would be raped? Of course. But it was not safe. I did it because my boyfriend was there and because I thought the other boys there were my friends.

Obviously, I thought wrong.

The morning I woke up in my car outside Brian's house, I took a long shower at Adriana's, hoping it would clear my head, but I was still sick as a dog when I got out. I couldn't seem to get my brain straight. The lump on my head had become truly alarming and had grown to the size of an egg, and no amount of Tylenol would make it stop pulsing with pain. I fell into Adriana's bed and passed out for another three hours. This was no ordinary hangover; I could barely open my eyes, and I couldn't remember anything. Later, those symptoms would lead me to believe that I might have been drugged. But at the time, I had no idea what was wrong with me.

When I awoke, Adriana's mom was there—and she was furious.

She was almost a second mom to me, and I found myself squirming under her scrutiny. She had a million questions: Why was I there? Why was I sleeping in the middle of the afternoon? What had happened to my head? Even without matted vomit in my hair, I still looked incredibly rough. Adriana's mom accused me of partying all night and then using her home to get cleaned up before going home. "This isn't a hotel," she informed me, in no uncertain terms.

It was like I'd woken up in a *Twilight Zone* episode. It was four o'clock in the afternoon, and I felt muzzy and confused. Adriana's mom's questions were making me panic; I didn't have any answers for her. The worst part was that Adriana—my best friend, my closest ally, my sister—still didn't believe that anything had happened to me.

I got scared that Adriana's mom would call my parents, who thought I'd gone to Six Flags, so I convinced Adriana to leave the house with me. Our friend Melaney lived about four houses down, so we went there.

Melaney opened the door, took one look at me, and said, "Oh my God. What happened to you? What on earth did you do last night?"

I gave her the same answer I'd given Brian's mom and Adriana: "I don't remember." I told her I'd driven down to Seth's beach house the night before. I'd had a beer, one hit of weed, and remembered sitting on the couch and talking to Seth when Jared made me a drink. The next thing I remembered was waking up in my car around the corner from Brian's house. I told her about my bra falling out of my jeans when I went to take a shower, about the blood, and about Jared's disturbing comment to me on the phone.

Unlike Adriana, Melaney didn't try to tell me I was crazy. She didn't try to convince me that the guys we knew couldn't have done something so heinous. I could see right away that she'd come to the same conclusion I had: Something had happened, and it hadn't been good.

But what she said next surprised me. She said, "Have you prayed?"

Melaney's family was extremely religious, and she was, too. But it wasn't a topic she talked about with her friends, so her question startled me. Adriana wasn't religious, and neither was I. My mom had been raised as a Christian, in a fairly devout household. Her grandfather was a pastor, but practicing Christianity went out the window when she met my dad, who is Jewish.

My dad doesn't go to temple or celebrate any Jewish

holiday except Hanukkah, but he does feel Jewish—in no small part because his own grandfather had survived a concentration camp and lived with one of the hateful numbers tattooed on his wrist. Grandpa had hit the roof when he'd found out my dad was dating a woman who wasn't Jewish and swore he wouldn't attend the wedding unless my mom agreed to convert. She knew that she'd never be welcome in her husband's family home unless she did, so she said she would. But after their wedding, she found she couldn't do it. She wasn't a regular at church anymore, but her Christianity felt too important to her, too central to her understanding of herself, to throw away.

My dad's parents had already fallen in love with my mom, so the conversion issue was dropped. But her Christianity remained deeply private, and my brother and I were raised to think of ourselves as Jewish, though we never learned anything about Judaism or celebrated any holidays except Hanukkah. We were raised with an understanding of God, though, and of the power of prayer. I had been born premature, and my parents always told me that God had heard their prayers and saved their miracle baby's life. So although I wasn't raised with any formal religion, I always prayed, and I knew that there was a God.

Still, Melaney's comment that afternoon—"Have you prayed?"—startled me. I was struck by how natural and immediate it had been for her to reach for prayer in a moment of crisis. It was a reflex for her. I felt so frightened and unhappy and alone, and for one fleeting moment, I wished for a relationship with God that would bring me comfort.

But that afternoon, I just shook my head. I hadn't prayed. It would never have occurred to me, for starters. And I didn't know how.

Then the moment passed, and Melaney spoke again. "But you don't know that anything happened for sure, right?"

Of course I didn't. I didn't know anything! To her credit, Melaney never said—as Adriana had—"No way, those guys wouldn't do that." But the hard look on Melaney's face when she said "Even if they did what you think they did, you can't prove it" was unforgettable.

She was right. Hanging in the air was the unspoken understanding that Seth's dad was extremely wealthy and powerful. These weren't people to mess with.

Adriana and Melaney's reactions were, in essence, the same reactions that I would confront over and over in the years to follow. Adriana's automatic response was, "No way. These are good guys, guys we know. You just got drunk." Either the guys hadn't done anything, or I'd somehow asked for what happened to me by getting so wasted.

Melaney's response was even more cynical. She was essentially saying, "Even if you were raped, there's nothing that can be done about it. The best thing you can do? Brush it under the rug, pretend it didn't happen."

Those first, knee-jerk responses were only the beginning of the betrayals I would suffer at the hands of my friends. They (and many others) would go on to pressure me to drop the case and then testify against me. They were themselves under a tremendous amount of pressure. But it was sad—and telling about the way young women are taught to think about rape—that two teenaged girls responded the way they did. These were my best friends, girls who knew better than anyone that I was reliable, punctual, loyal to a fault. There I was in front of them, disoriented, bleeding, frightened, covered in bruises. Why were they so sure that nothing had happened—and that if it had, nothing could be done?

It was only a matter of time before my parents discovered my whereabouts. My mom had killer instincts, especially where I was concerned, and she hadn't bought the Six Flags story at all. She kept calling and pushing me. "Why do you sound so out of it? It's pretty quiet for an amusement park. How come I don't hear any roller coasters?" I'd reassured her that we were calling from a bathroom at the park, but she wasn't buying it. "Where are you, Alisa? I want you to come home. Tell me where you are, and we'll come pick you up. What's going on?"

The pressure was starting to get to me, and my head pounded as if about to explode. I hung up; she called back. I didn't pick up; she called back again. And again, and again, and again. When it became clear to her that I wasn't going to pick up, she and my dad got in the car to look for me.

On their way over to Adriana's, they passed Melaney's house and saw my car in the driveway. When I saw their car pull up, I hid in Melaney's pantry. My parents were knocking at the windows—my dad had climbed the back fence—and ringing the doorbell. Finally, Melaney got worried that her own parents were going to come home to this craziness and she forced me to come out. I was busted. My parents already knew that I'd lied. There was nothing to do but face the music.

My parents threw me in the backseat of their car, and my dad drove my car home. As soon as we got there, they sat me down at the kitchen table. It was truth-telling time.

After sixteen years of being the good girl, this should have been the worst moment of my life. But my brain was so occupied by my steadily increasing suspicion that these boys I knew and trusted had done something unimaginably horrible to me, and my growing realization of what it would mean if I had been raped, that my parents' anger hardly registered. To be honest, it even felt a little bit good to know that I was in trouble. At least the adults were in charge now.

I told my parents I'd lied to them. We hadn't gone to Six Flags at all. I'd gone out to spend the night with my boyfriend at his beach house.

My mom cried, but my dad, his face grim, stayed focused. The next question, I guess, was inevitable: "Have you been having sex?"

Again, if you'd asked me the week before, I would have told you that having this conversation with my parents—simply hearing my father say the word *sex*—would be my number-one worst nightmare. But another, fresher, and more terrifying fear was beginning to percolate up through my confusion. If I'd had sex the night before without realizing it, I could be pregnant. I could have an STD. I could have AIDS. If I couldn't trust those boys not to have had sex with me when I was too drunk or stoned to remember it, I could hardly rely on them to have used protection.

In one moment, I saw every single one of my dreams go up in smoke. If I was pregnant or sick, there would be no New York, no college, no journalism school, no changing the world. This was real, enormous, something I couldn't fix.

I nodded. Yes. I'd been having sex. And no, we hadn't used protection.

The very idea that I was sexually active sent a tremendous shock wave through the whole family. My parents didn't know I had a boyfriend. They'd never heard of Seth or Brian. But they did exactly what I thought they would do: They put me right back in the car and we drove down to the hospital. The doctor gave me antibiotics in case I'd contracted an STD and the morning-after pill. But everyone was assuming that the sex had been consensual, and I didn't say different. So the emergency room doctors didn't give me a proper Sexual Assault Response Team (SART) exam. This would be harmful to my case during the trial.

The drive home from the hospital was miserable. My parents were furious with me. We were so close that even in an ordinary situation this would have made me feel sad and alone. But I was so scared and confused that their anger felt completely intolerable to me. On the drive home, I had a fantasy of laying my head down in my mother's lap so she could stroke my hair and tell me that everything was all right. But that would mean telling her what I suspected, and I was nowhere near ready to do that. And I was beginning to suspect that whatever trouble I'd gotten into was bigger than even my mom could fix.

My dad was on the warpath, angrier than I'd ever seen him. When we got home, he made me give him Brian's number and the number of the boy I'd lost my virginity to. He called both of them and told them, in no uncertain terms, that they were to keep away from me. He called Seth's dad, too, and told him that underaged kids had been drinking and having sex under his roof. Then he read me the riot act and took my car keys. I was grounded until further notice.

I still had no idea what had happened to me.

I wasn't spacey anymore, but I was keyed up beyond belief. With my stomach roiling from the adrenaline coursing through my system, I walked into my beloved childhood bedroom. I'd covered the whole closet wall with a collage I'd made of photographs of my friends, along with greeting cards, stickers, and meaningful words and phrases cut from magazines. The project had taken me the better part of a year, and it was still a work in progress.

There was so much love and fun and hope on that wall. But that day, as soon as I walked into my room, I felt an overwhelming urge to flee. The faces looking out at me from those photographs seemed malevolent. There was Adriana, my best friend, my sister, practically—who hadn't believed me. There was Melaney, who had believed me, but whose response had basically been that I was powerless and should pretend it hadn't happened. Worst of all, there were Seth and Brian, grinning out at me from my own walls. The sight of their faces made my stomach lurch. I'd thought they were my friends. What had they done?

I looked at all those quotes and phrases I'd so painstakingly collected and cut out. *Fearless. Light up. Beautiful dream.* I'd loved to lie on my bed, getting inspired by those words. I'd think about the life I would make for myself in New York and how proud my parents would be of me.

Other moms couldn't wait to plan their daughters' weddings, but my mom had told me over and over again that she couldn't wait to see me cross the stage in gown and mortarboard on the day of my graduation. As sick as I felt about everything that had happened with my friends, the worst thought was that I'd let her—and myself—down. I couldn't believe I'd jeopardized all my precious dreams by putting myself in this position. I'd known that I shouldn't have gone out to that beach house. I'd had a bad feeling, a premonition, almost. But I'd ignored it, and now here I was, facing a crisis of such enormity I couldn't begin to wrap my head around it.

Looking at that collage was like standing in the ocean and seeing a massive wave crest up in front of you, the moment when you realize that there is absolutely nothing you can do to get out of its way. I wanted desperately to run— to run away from the situation, to run away from myself. The sentiments on that wall seemed to belong to a different time, a different girl.

I could see it very clearly: My life had changed, and nothing on that wall had anything to do with me anymore.

I would have no control over what came next. Whether I liked it or not, I would be swept up, tossed around, and then slammed to the ground.

*True Hearts.* That phrase was pasted next to a picture of me with Melaney and Adriana. With a heart as sick as my stomach, I waited to hear the familiar sounds of my parents getting ready for bed. Then I grabbed my pillow and headed off to the family room to sleep on the couch.

## CHAPTER TWO

# *A Series of Shocks*

I was sleeping on the couch three days later when our phone rang at five thirty in the morning.

My father picked up.

It was the police, looking for my grandfather. My grandfather had died a few weeks before, but my cell phone plan was in his name, so that's who they asked for.

My father was completely disoriented. What on earth could the police want with my dead grandfather at five thirty in the morning?

The caller clarified: "We're trying to locate Alisa Kaplan."

"That's my daughter. Do you want to tell me what's going on?"

"This is Detective John Houston. We have a video here that we need to discuss with her. Is your daughter in the house?"

Alarm growing, my dad got out of bed and started

moving down the hallway toward my room. "She's asleep, safe and sound, in her bed. Is she in trouble? What's going on?"

The detective kept pressing. "She hasn't been in the hospital recently? No injuries? She's healthy?"

My dad was beginning to freak out. "Let me get her, and we'll talk about this together." He broke into a run and threw open my bedroom door. Then he screamed.

My bed, of course, was empty. I'd been sleeping in the family room for three nights, because I couldn't bear sleeping under that collage. But I'd kept my sleep arrangements a secret. If my parents knew I wasn't sleeping in my cherished bedroom, they'd start asking questions, and I didn't have any answers to give them. So I'd sneak off to the couch in the family room after they turned in, and I'd wake up when I heard my dad turning off the alarm system in the morning. While he was letting the dogs out, I'd disappear down the hall, back to my bedroom.

The scream woke me, and I sat bolt upright on the couch.

"Alisa, where are you?"

"Dad, I'm in here!" He stumbled in, clutching the phone, and told the detective he'd found me.

The room was still dark; the sun hadn't come up yet. My dad turned on the light and kneeled next to the couch. My mother came into the room, confused and frightened, still rubbing the sleep from her eyes.

"Who's on the phone, Rick?"

But my dad held up a hand and spoke again to John

Houston. "What's on this videotape that you need to discuss with Alisa?"

"We have recovered a videotape, shot on the fifth of July, of a person we believe to be your daughter. We suspect that she may have been involved in a gang rape."

I couldn't hear what the detective had said, but I was inches away, watching my dad's face. When a person dies, it's sometimes said that you can see the life leave their eyes. That was what happened to my father: His face went blank, as if the soul had been stripped right out of him. For a moment, it was as if my father wasn't there at all.

That look frightened me as much or more than anything that had happened up to that point. I had no idea what the person on the other end of the line had said to make his face go blank like that, but I burst into tears, my whole body shaking as if I were having a seizure. My dad grabbed my hand and said, "Alisa, I need you to be honest with me. It's very important. I need you to tell me the truth. Where were you on July fifth and sixth?"

I said, "I told you, Daddy. I was at Seth's beach house. I promise, I was at Seth's beach house."

"Alisa, I need you to tell me what happened. You have to tell me exactly what happened that night."

I was crying so hard I could barely get the words out. "I swear, Daddy, I don't know. I just don't know."

That was the first time in my life that I ever saw my dad cry.

My poor mom didn't have the slightest idea what was happening, but she was watching me and my dad, and

25

she could tell that something unbelievably horrendous had taken place.

"Rick, tell me what it is," she begged, and my father, his face wet with tears, turned around and looked at her. Very plainly and clearly he said, "The police say Alisa may have been gang-raped."

That was the first time I heard those words. Immediately, my stomach clenched, and I started to throw up. I was shaking so badly that my knees were collapsing out from underneath me, so my parents grabbed me on either side and carried me into the bathroom.

As I rested my head on the cool porcelain, I could hear my father, still on the phone with the detective. "She says she doesn't know what happened."

There wasn't anything more they could tell us over the phone. "You need to come down to the station immediately."

I don't remember getting dressed, but ten minutes later, I was sitting in the backseat of my parents' car.

All three of us were crying. I told them every detail I could remember about the night at Seth's house. It wasn't much, but I felt hugely relieved to get whatever I knew out there. My parents were completely amazing; both of them made a special point to tell me how much they loved and supported me. "Whatever happened, we'll get through this together, as a family."

They did have one question: Why hadn't I told them what I suspected had happened? In this, too, I told them the truth: "I didn't want to get anyone in trouble without having proof."

It was crazy, but driving over to the station with them as the sun came up that morning, I felt almost happy. From my perspective, the worst was over. Though my fears about the rape had been confirmed, I no longer had to carry the terrible burden of my suspicions around with me. Plus, I wasn't alone. My parents knew what had happened to me, and they still loved me.

At heart, I was a good girl. With the exception of the previous few months, I was accustomed to enjoying a close relationship with my family. My mom seems tiny and fragile, but she's always been the glue that holds our family together, and I knew she'd do whatever she had to in order to get us through this. And my dad, the big, strong, silent ex-cop, had always been there to protect his little girl.

We would take this next step together.

Almost immediately, however, we were caught up in a whirlwind that none of us could understand or control. At the station, my parents went one way, into one interview room. I went to another.

The deputies couldn't tell us very much, but we were able to piece together some of the story from what they told us and, later, from testimony at trial. The deputies had gotten hold of a videotape Seth had made. He'd taken his video camera to another beach house and left it there. When someone at *that* beach house saw what was on it, she decided to hide the camera and tape in her car, and later she gave it to a friend of hers, who turned it over to the police.

After they did, it had taken the police a while to find me. Why? They'd begun their search for the anonymous girl in the video not with Seth's friends, but in the local morgues. They believed from what they'd seen that I was dead.

Not a day goes by that I don't think about the woman who turned in the tape. She stands for everything that is good in humanity. It would have been so easy for her to turn a blind eye to what she saw on that videotape. Apparently, other people at that beach house had. But she put herself on the line for a girl she didn't even know, simply because she knew that what she was watching was wrong. That makes her a hero.

Much later, when I heard the parable of the Good Samaritan and finally understood where that expression came from, the woman who turned in the tape popped right into my head. In this Bible story, a man is robbed and beaten and left for dead. A priest passes his body and does not stop. Another citizen passes his body and does not stop. But then a Samaritan, one of the most hated groups in that society, happens to pass by, and he does stop. Not only does the Samaritan comfort the victim, but he cleans and dresses his wounds, and then brings him to an inn, where he pays for his food and shelter. Before he leaves, he instructs the innkeeper to take care of the wounded man and promises to pay whatever extra is owed on his way back.

For me, it's one of the most powerful stories in the Bible. We could use more Good Samaritans, that's for sure. In 2012, in Steubenville, Ohio, a high school girl was sexually assaulted by a number of her peers. The similarities between her case and mine are striking. She was also incapacitated—drunk or drugged past consent. Her assault was also videotaped and shared. (Thank God there was no Twitter in 2002.) Her assailants, stars on the football team in a sports-obsessed town, were immediately defended as "good guys" by the community, while her "bad girl" history of sexual promiscuity was paraded for the courts and the press. (In fairness, there were a couple of dedicated, passionate journalists who stood up to the defense's publicity team in my own case, including the award-winning investigative reporter Scott Moxley of the *OC Weekly*.)

Needless to say, I followed the Steubenville case closely, and I went so far as to clip out an interview with Steubenville police chief William McCafferty. For a long while, I kept it taped above my desk. In it he says, "The thing I found most disturbing about this is that there were other people around when this was going on. Nobody had the morals to say, 'Hey, stop it, that isn't right.' If you could charge people for not being decent human beings, a lot of people could have been charged that night."

That is such a powerful idea! If one person, possessing a little courage, had stood up that night in Steubenville, they could have changed the course of that young woman's life, just as the Good Samaritan saved the life of the robbed man.

Not everyone was comfortable with what was happening that night in Steubenville. In the background of one of the leaked videos, you can hear at least one boy trying to rein his friends in. But he didn't act. Imagine what would have happened if he had!

I believe, in my case, that the women who turned in the tape are precisely the decent human beings that Police Chief McCafferty was talking about. I don't use the word *hero* lightly. It's hard to buck peer pressure and do the right thing when it would be so much easier to close your eyes and wish the ugliness away. Good Samaritans, like the woman who turned in the tape, give me hope every day.

But I had no thought for the woman who'd turned in the tape of my assault that first morning down at the station. All I felt was panic, and a growing feeling of terrible dread.

The deputies indicated that all three of my friends had been involved, but nobody was responding to my questions and requests for more information. What exactly had they done?

I heard the deputies talking about arrests and search warrants, and I desperately wished I could wave a magic wand and make the whole situation go away. Whatever had happened, the guys had been drunk. They hadn't been thinking straight. These were my friends—I didn't want to get them in trouble.

The deputies asked me to identify parts of my body from still screen shots taken from the video. It was disturbing to see these pictures of myself, cut up into parts like a bucket of fried chicken. There was a shot of my hair, one of part of my belly and torso. It was definitely me.

Then they told me that I'd need to get down to the hospital for a SART exam. No way, I said. I'd showered compulsively in the three days since whatever had happened. Any evidence that might have been there had long been washed down the drain.

The detective explained that I probably had injuries and marks on the inside of my body from what they'd done to me. "If this is prosecuted," she kept saying, "we'll need this evidence."

I finally agreed to go. The detective told me that I'd have a victim's advocate there the whole time. I could trust the advocate, she reassured me.

When we got to the hospital, my victim's advocate, Tiare, was waiting outside. I was impressed. She'd gotten there early so she could be there with me every step of the way. I was also impressed by her gorgeous, long, thick hair and her huge smile. Tiare very clearly explained her role: "I support sexual assault survivors and their families." It was the first time I had heard the word *survivor* used in reference to sexual assault, and it gave me a little lift. Apparently, this experience could be survived.

Tiare stayed with me every step of the way, as she'd told me she would. But the SART exam was still terrifying.

The hospital had a special room set up for the exam, which is videotaped so that what they find can be used as evidence. When I saw the camera and the instruments, I started to freak out. I was sixteen—I'd never even had a regular gynecological exam.

But Tiare stayed very calm and collected, and kept it positive. She talked in a sweet, low voice, and I focused on her words. Yes, it would be uncomfortable, but it wouldn't be that uncomfortable, and anyway it wouldn't take long, and I was so brave, and she'd be right there with me.

"If there's anything you don't want to do, you say the word," Tiare told me over and over again. It was important to me to feel I had some control. She also distracted me by getting me to talk about what I liked to do for fun—so I told her all about my car and where I liked to drive it. The nurse was great, too, and told me every single thing she was going to do. Tiare explained why every procedure was necessary, but even with her experienced ministrations, I was shaking so hard at some points that the nurse had to wait to continue with the exam.

As the exam went on, I found myself getting increasingly anxious. Mostly, I needed some confirmation that all of this had happened because none of it felt real. Finally, I asked the nurse, "Do you see anything?"

She nodded and then said, very simply, "There are a lot of rips and tears."

When I heard that, I got really, really scared.

Afterward, Tiare hugged me and told me how great I'd been. "If the DA decides to prosecute, you'll have helped them out with important evidence," she told me. Until that moment, it hadn't occurred to me that my ordeal wouldn't end when the SART exam did.

My parents drove me home. We were all wrung out and exhausted by the events of the day, and I fell into bed without dinner, but I found I couldn't sleep. The idea of prosecution and a trial loomed up ahead like a bogeyman in the dark. I thought about what Tiare had said. The cops had talked about prosecution, too. What did that mean? Was there nothing I could do to stop this, even if I wanted to?

I collect little figurines of angels now. My friends and family gave most of them to me. These little figurines hang mostly in my bedroom, where they give me comfort. They make me feel that I am safe and protected, no matter what might happen. And that was how Tiare made me feel, as she sat behind me, soothing me with her voice and stroking my hair. I always say that she was my first angel.

Her calming presence that day has everything to do with why I became a victim's advocate myself. Every time I sit behind a survivor during a SART exam, rubbing her shoulders and holding her shaking hand, I think about Tiare and what it meant to me, during the darkest hour of my life, to have her calm, strong, sweet, supportive presence behind me.

Because of the way I'd felt the next morning and the fact I couldn't remember anything that had happened at the beach house, I couldn't shake the feeling that the drink Jared had made me had been laced. Of course, we couldn't prove it. All traces of any drug would have been gone from my bloodstream by the time the police finally found me, three days later.

On top of all this, I still didn't know exactly what had happened to me. My parents must have had a more finely attuned sense of what they could tolerate; I don't think they even asked. So three days later, when our golden retriever, Brandy, returned from the bottom of the driveway as she did every morning, tail wagging and the freshly delivered newspaper in her mouth, none of us were prepared for what we saw splashed across the front page: a detailed description of the gang rape charges that had been filed.

A press release from the prosecutor's office was even more explicit. My three friends had had vaginal, anal, and oral sex with my unconscious body, first on a couch, then on a pool table. They slapped and pinched me, and made signs to each other that I was still out cold. They continued for more than forty minutes while making hand signs pretending they were gangsters, laughing, and mugging for the camera while they assaulted me with the thick end of a pool cue, a Snapple bottle, a juice can, and a lit cigarette.

I didn't make it to the bathroom before I threw up, and neither did my mom.

# CHAPTER THREE

## *Harassed*

S eth, Brian, and Jared were charged with twenty-four felony charges, including rape and assault with a deadly weapon.

The DA's office asked me if I'd testify. That was a nice way of putting it; really, they told me that I was expected to testify. I didn't want to. In fact, with every fiber of my being, I wanted this whole thing to go away. But the DA's office very clearly told me that they were planning to go ahead with the trial, and that I would almost certainly be called, whether I wanted to testify or not. It would be easier for everyone if I cooperated with them.

The wheels were set in motion.

Immediately, it became clear that Seth's dad was serious about making sure the case didn't come to trial. He was astronomically rich and hugely influential in county politics. (The alarming corruption in the sheriff's department would come to light later, in large part because of my case.

The only reason Seth's dad didn't do time in prison himself was because he testified against his friends.)

I hadn't been named in any of the papers, but the harassment began as soon as the DA's office announced they'd try the case. One day when my mom was leaving for work, she saw a dark green SUV sitting at the end of our block. My parents lived in a quiet suburb. People parked in their garages, so any car that was parked on the street drew attention—particularly if the man in the car was taking notes and stayed there from morning until night.

We started seeing that same car frequently around our neighborhood. About a week later, my mom saw the guy talking to our neighbor, Beverley. When she asked what he wanted, he told Beverley he was a private investigator hired by the district attorney's office to investigate a rape that had allegedly taken place. But when my mom checked, the DA's office had never heard of him.

After that, there was almost always a car parked outside our house. If we called the cops, the guy outside would drive off and come back later. I was frightened and confused. What were they looking for, and why? Why were they watching me? I hadn't done anything wrong, had I?

My parents were understandably freaked out. They perceived, more quickly than I did, that my safety might be at risk, and they started circling the wagons. I wasn't ever allowed to be home by myself. If my parents had to go out, they made sure that my brother would be home. If he had plans, I had to go wherever they were going.

Then, on a sunny afternoon at the end of July, I got

a really bad scare. I was making my way home from the tanning salon when I noticed a maroon Volvo following me. The man inside was driving very aggressively, tailgating me so closely I felt sure he was about to slam into my car. Then he pulled up next to me at a light and started photographing me with a large, official-looking camera, like the paparazzi that had chased Princess Diana to her death.

I was terrified. I tried to get away from him, but no matter how fast I drove or how quickly I turned, he was always right behind me. In a panic, I called my mom. She was even more frightened than I was. Neither of us had any idea who he was or what he was likely to do. She got on the house phone to the police department. By the time she got a cop on the phone, she was practically losing her mind with fear for me.

In the meantime, I was screaming and crying into the speakerphone and driving like a maniac, trying everything I could think of to get this car off my tail. It's a miracle that I didn't die in an accident that day. I was a good driver (my dad had made sure of that), but an inexperienced one; I was sixteen, after all. Yet there I was, driving as if I were doing stunts on a closed course.

The police told my mom to tell me to go to the police station. I'd never been there before, so she had to give me directions. Between her own nerves and my hysteria, I barely made it. But they didn't think to mention that there were two entrances. I took the turn into the wrong one, and the guy in the Volvo followed me in, blocking me in so I couldn't get out. Then he was out of the car, running toward me with the camera up and flashing, shooting picture after picture of me trapped in my car, powerless to do anything but scream in fear and outrage.

Eventually, my mom was able to figure out what had happened, and a number of police officers came around back to find me. As soon as he saw the cops approach, the guy jumped back into his car and reversed out of there. I was a shaking mess, so frightened I could hardly speak, let alone drive. Being stalked, chased, cornered, and photographed like that had left me more vulnerable and scared than I have ever been.

The incident completely traumatized me. My car had been my happy place. In the months immediately after they'd given it to me, my parents had laughed about how easy it was to get me to run errands for them—as long as I could crank up the radio and zoom around, I'd gladly run out to pick up coals for the barbecue or whatever they needed. But after the incident that ended up at the police station, I felt shaky and scared as soon as I had the keys in my hand. I didn't like to be in the car by myself at all anymore. Even if someone was with me, as soon as I got behind the wheel, I made sure the windows were rolled up and checked the mirrors compulsively for a tail. My days of cruising for fun and relaxation were over.

The incident had also completely traumatized my parents. As a result, they got more and more controlling. One day, my dad yelled at me for simply sitting at the window in my room, looking out at the street. "They're going to take your picture!" he yelled. I started to accuse him of paranoia, but, as usual, there was a car parked outside. Plus, the DA's office knew that my resolve to testify was wavering, and they may have been worried that I would run away, yet another reason for my parents to keep close tabs on me. More and more, I was trapped in my room.

A side effect of rape is the feeling of powerlessness, of a loss of control. For me, everything that came afterward seemed to exacerbate that feeling.

My parents were trying to protect me, but it was a difficult thing for me to tolerate. I was supposed to be coming into my own, becoming a young woman. Precisely when I should be experiencing independence for the first time, I had round-the-clock babysitting instead. It was a blow to my emerging sense of myself.

The press, meanwhile, had gone crazy. Seth's dad's money and influence, combined with the shocking nature of the crime, made the story headline fodder—and not only in California, but all over the world. Seth's dad responded immediately by hiring a full-time publicist.

That's probably why so many of the news stories focused on the impact that the case would have on these "good boys." These hardworking, upstanding young men from good families had made a mistake, more than one article claimed. Should their whole lives be derailed because they'd gotten a little drunk? Why should these smart, gentle boys have their lives ruined because of one dumb girl?

I was shocked. I was incredibly naïve, and it had not yet

occurred to me how many different ways you can tell—or spin—a story. The worst part was that, deep down, I agreed.

I'd like to tell you that I read those stories and got out-raged and angry. Sometimes I did. But more often, I took them at face value and let what they were saying reinforce everything I was already feeling, so that I saw myself as even more worthless than I had felt already.

People tend to be shocked when they hear about the bias in the reporting that was done on my case. The sad truth is that victim blaming in the press is common, not just in my case, but in lots of rape cases. In 2011, the *New York Times* reported on the gang rape of an eleven-year-old girl. The writer described the girl as "dressed older than her age, wearing makeup and fashions more appropriate to a woman in her 20s." She hung out with teenagers, the writer made sure to mention.

Read between the lines, and the message is clear: She was asking for it.

This is classic victim blaming. The simple truth is that, no matter what she was wearing or doing, or what her reputation was (and remember, we're talking about an eleven-year-old girl!), she did not deserve to be gang-raped.

Later in the article, the writer quoted one of the people in the town: "The boys have to live with this the rest of their lives." When I see a similar comment now, I think, *Yes, hopefully, they will have to live with it for the rest of their lives. And if you don't want to live with the consequences of being a sexual predator, then you probably shouldn't go around raping people.*

When similar things were being written about me, though, I was too devastated to be rational.

That summer, I saw my dreams of being a journalist circle the drain. I'd always thought about journalists as heroes who did a public service by exposing injustice and shining light on the stories of the underrepresented. More than anything, I had wanted to be the next Barbara Walters. I loved how smart she was, how hard-hitting, how uncompromising in her dedication to the story. She didn't back down from controversy or let the rich and powerful intimidate her. Nothing was more important than getting to the truth.

But the reporters writing about my case were essentially printing the press releases that the defense handed them. This was how they used the power they'd been given? This wasn't journalism; it was publicity. The only thing I could console myself with was my anonymity: At least in the articles, I was referred to as Jane Doe.

Then an acquaintance from around the neighborhood called my mom.

"I am so sorry to hear about what happened to Alisa," she said.

We had told very few people what was going on, and the woman who called was nowhere near my mom's inner circle. My mom says that when she heard that, the hackles stood up on the back of her neck.

"What do you mean?" she asked.

Our neighbor had found a bright orange flier in her mailbox, which read: "IMPORTANT NOTICE: Anyone having information regarding the Kaplan family and/or the circumstances concerning the alleged rape of their daughter on or about July 6, 2002, please call."

The number led to Seth's mother's voice mail box. She denied having anything to do with it.

Legally, the victim in a sexual assault case is guaranteed privacy, especially a minor. But the entire neighborhood had been papered in the bright orange fliers. They were posted on every community bulletin board in the area, pushed under doors and into mailboxes, and taped in the windows of local businesses.

My brother, Jaime, went to each and every one of those stores and restaurants, and ripped each and every one of those fliers down. The lady who delivered our mail took them out of mailboxes whenever she saw them and reported the incident to her bosses. But the damage had already been done. I was living in a community of 170,000 people spread out over forty square miles, and this was one of the most scandalous things that had ever happened there. There was nowhere to hide. My time as a Jane Doe was over.

By the end of July, because of the intense media attention on the case and the smear campaign, everyone in my town knew what had happened to me. (More than I did, probably, considering my parents forbade me to read any account that might have details we hadn't already heard.) I endured shaming whispers behind hands at the dry cleaners, the grocery store, the bowling alley. There was nowhere to hide. Suddenly, I was "the girl who'd cried rape."

A couple of years ago, a friend asked me why rape victims feel shame. I opened my mouth to bite her head off, and then I stopped. It's actually a good question. "I can understand that you'd feel violated," she continued. "But why shame? It's not as if you did anything wrong. Why should you feel like you did?"

It made me think: Why is there so much shame associated with rape? I think a lot of it comes out of the way we persist in blaming the victim. This is the idea that you must have done something to ask for it or it wouldn't have happened, right?

It's hard to understand why people feel the need to do this, but for me it all fell into perspective when a friend told me that when her grandmother was a girl, it was common to whisper the word *cancer*. Seventy years ago, cancer was considered to be a shameful condition. Nice people didn't talk about it.

I was astounded when I heard that for the first time. Why on earth would there be stigma associated with cancer? But I now believe that people whispered the word for the same reason they blame rape victims. Rape and cancer are both misfortunes that can (and do) happen to anyone. But nobody wants to think that those things can happen to them, so they comfort themselves by blaming the victim. If they want to believe it can't happen to them, then they have to believe that there was a reason that it happened to you.

It may not be admirable, but it's human.

The good news is that we don't whisper the word *cancer* anymore. Survivors and their supporters proudly wear pink ribbons and Livestrong bracelets, and march together to fund research. It's my hope that if we keep pointing out how wrong victim blaming is, and how it hurts rape victims, then sexual assault survivors will get there, too. We still have a ways to go, though, and as a survivor I can tell you that the sense of shame is real—and it is a terrible thing to live with on a daily basis.

As the summer progressed, the harassment got more intense with every passing day. My dad was routinely followed to work and photographed. One guy called our house, offering his services to investigate our side of the case. We discovered that he was already working for the defense; the call had been a troll for information. One night my brother woke up to a noise outside the house. When he got up to investigate, he found that it wasn't a raccoon raiding our trash, but a strange man nosing through the coffee grounds and carrot peels. The whole family felt violated.

Then a copy of my cell phone records showed up in the mail—"per our request," said the accompanying letter.

But we hadn't requested any phone records. Someone else had, apparently. It was deeply disturbing to realize that they'd had whatever security information they needed to get the records released. The same thing happened with my medical records, never mind that neither of my parents had signed for their release. We found out when the publicist for the defense handed them out—my private medical records. Nothing was safe.

One other circumstance that summer hurt me worse than all of the fear and intimidation and humiliation did, or the loss of my independence: I no longer had anywhere to go, or anyone to go with. I had lost all of my friends.

Right after the charges were pressed, the phone rang off the hook. One after another, my girlfriends called me to ask me to reconsider my testimony. Seth and Brian were good guys, they told me. They'd been drunk. The guys hadn't known what they were doing. I'd been drunk, too. And besides, they were quick to remind me, it wasn't as if I'd been some pristine virgin. I bore some responsibility in this, too.

Private investigators had gotten to them. I believed this because my friend Beka told me. She told me they'd tried to get to her and her family, too. Beka and I had been friends since fifth grade. She was upbeat and spunky, with the most contagious laugh you've ever heard. And while she liked to have a good time, she wasn't a party girl and didn't hang out with them, either.

She told me investigators had shown up at her house, hoping that since Beka was such a good friend of mine, maybe she could help me see what a silly idea it would be to testify. Certainly we'd both be very well taken care of; we could have anything we wanted. Beka's parents were allies: They told us about the offers they'd received. Their family, though, was the exception to the rule. As it became clear that I wasn't going to be pressured into not testifying, the phone stopped ringing. Aside from Beka, my friends were just gone.

There was no one to talk to, no one to tell me a joke, no one to hug me, no one to eat ice cream with. I was, of course, lucky enough to have the unconditional support of my family. But ask any sixteen-year-old girl, and she'll tell you that her friends mean the world to her, and I was no different. Those girls and I had been inseparable. We'd shared everything: clothes, makeup, notes for class. We knew each other's locker combinations and hopes for the future. Now, suddenly, I'd been cut from the herd.

The next thing I heard about my girlfriends came from the DA's office. They would be testifying against me. I'm not sure there are words to describe how much this hurt.


You've probably heard about a number of cases recently where girls have killed themselves after being sexually assaulted. In almost every case, it's clear that the decision to die by suicide had less to do with the sexual assault than with the online shaming these girls had to endure after the rape: pictures of the assault posted on Twitter, public bullying via Facebook. I have a hard enough time understanding how boys could bully a rape victim after the fact, but it makes me absolutely crazy to know that girls—many of them their former friends—attacked the victims, too, calling them sluts and liars.

What is it that makes girls turn on one another? More victim blaming, I suppose. I thank God every day that there was no Facebook or Twitter yet the summer I was raped. I lived through the pre-digital version, though, and I can completely understand why those girls killed themselves: the harassment, the name-calling, the cruelty, and the betrayal by their so-called friends.

Even my parents' friends faded away. Many of them simply didn't know what to say. One woman had the audacity to tell my mother that she didn't want her own daughter to hang out with me because she felt it would increase her daughter's chance of getting raped, as if what had happened to me was contagious.

At the end of the summer, I tried to organize a group of girls to go to the L.A. County Fair. We'd always loved to do that, and I was desperate for some normal teenage fun. I left voice mail messages, but nobody called me back. Beka was the only person who showed up to go with me.

That night, when we got back from the fair, I took my fingernails to the collage on my wall. Overtaken by a sudden, horrible fury, I clawed and scratched at my friends' faces and the inspirational phrases I'd so carefully pasted there, until my fingers bled and I finally collapsed in exhaustion on the floor of my room, surrounded by the shredded confetti of my dreams.

At least I still had Beka.

Then, early in the fall, she called me, her voice breaking. She told me that an investigator had figured out that she left for the bus stop in the morning after her parents had left for work, and had followed her. She was frightened: for herself, for her parents, for her little sister.

"Alisa, I can't keep going like this. I'm so sorry. But until this is over, I don't think I can see you anymore."

It must have been a terribly hard phone call to make, and I respected her for making it. At least she'd had the guts to call. Still, the fact remained that she'd been my last friend. I was truly alone.

I've thought a lot about my friends in the years since that summer and since I heard so many of them testify against me at my trial. I like to think that if the rape had happened to one of them, I would never have testified for the defense. Still, I don't hold it against them. I would have been terrified by the harassment, too, and I can't say that I wouldn't have withdrawn from the friendship. In any case, whether I understood their desertion or not, that summer was impossibly lonely and hard for me.

My days were spent meeting with detectives and lawyers and members of the district attorney's office. It felt like I spent most of them listening to my parents and adults in suits yelling about me as if I weren't there. I was sixteen and barely keeping my head above water, after all. But it was a profoundly disempowering experience to sit in those rooms with all those grown-ups, hearing them talk about me as if I weren't there.

A few months before, I had been a normal, healthy, active kid, an athlete surrounded by good friends. That summer, instead of heading off to the beach or the movies, I sat in my room by myself and cried. I'd stay up and watch TV at night, and then I'd sleep for most of the day, fifteen or sixteen hours at a stretch.

Falling asleep meant dropping into a delicious oblivion, a state of suspended animation where I was safe. Sleeping was the only time I wasn't acutely aware of being at the center of a humiliating, shameful circus I couldn't control.

By contrast, waking up was a hard slap in the face. There would be one glorious moment before I fully regained consciousness and remembered everything that was happening. Then, no matter how deeply I burrowed back under the covers, it would all come back to me in a rush. This wasn't simply some horrible nightmare I could shake off with a splash of water on my face. It was my life.

I kept a journal that summer. On August 22, I wrote:

*I still strongly believe that everything happens for a reason, but I'm really trying to figure out the reason for all this. Please let tomorrow be filled with only happiness! Please, God, show the meaning, help me understand? I pray for you to take this pain and confusion away, God. Bless me with peace in my thoughts. Thank you, God!*

Three days later I wrote:

*I am literally breaking down inside. This pain is tearing me apart. . . . I was reading an article in a magazine today about a rape victim. It really made me think when this is all over, I want to go around talking to teenage girls. . . . Maybe that's what this all meant. Maybe God wanted me to help people all along, but not the way I imagined or ever expected.*

Later that week I wrote:

*What would have happened to my family if I had died? It gives me goosebumps just thinking about it. They would never have been the same. I wonder what my life holds for me because I'm still on this earth to accomplish something. God kept me here for a reason. He wants me to do something good in my life. I just hope it all makes sense soon.*

The answers I was looking for continued to elude me. As August ended, I got increasingly anxious. I was still having a lot of distressing physical problems in the aftermath of the rape, including spotting, irregular periods, and quite a bit of pain. I spent a lot of time at the doctor's office as they tried to figure out whether I'd need surgery to correct the damage.

The thought of going back to school was nightmarish.

As painful as the summer's isolation had been, it was better than suspecting that every single person I passed in the hall or sat next to in algebra would be thinking about me lying on that pool table. Something as ordinary as running an everyday errand for my mother meant exposing myself to whispers behind hands, lewd comments made just quietly enough that they couldn't be heard by anyone else, hissed insults: "Slut!" "Whore!" "Tramp!" High school is a perfect incubator for cruelty. I didn't think I'd survive it.

So my parents consulted with my advocates at the district attorney's office, and they decided that I would start a different high school in September.

It wasn't an ideal situation: I'd imagined graduating with the friends I'd had since kindergarten, not starting over at a completely new and unfamiliar place. But I was coming to realize that those friends were gone, along with the old life I'd taken for granted. I would have to start over.

## CHAPTER FOUR

# *Chasing Oblivion*

B y the time the first day of my junior year rolled around, I had warmed to the idea of a fresh start at a new school. The defense's harassment of our family was still so intense that the DA's office thought it would be a good idea for me to start my new school using a different name. I chose Kylie, a name I'd always liked.

I'm an organization freak by nature, but I've never spent more time color-coding my school supplies than I did that year. Every notebook had a corresponding folder and highlighter set. The day before school started, I must have tried on and rejected a hundred outfits. I packed and repacked my bag over and over, checking a list to make sure I'd have everything I'd need. I went so far as to scrub my already immaculate car, both inside and out.

That night before bed, I prayed to be allowed to have a fresh start. After the first day of school, I wrote:

*I'm all smiles, and will not let tomorrow be any less of a day than today. I will keep my head up, my smile on, and my confidence in place tomorrow. If you want something bad enough, it will always happen.... I just wanted to say thanks to God because he completely answered my prayers last night. Only He knows what my tomorrow brings, but I will pray.*

Those first few weeks, I doubled down on my school-work and started to make some new friends. I was still struggling with depression, but getting my bearings at a new place and catching up on new schoolwork provided me with a truly welcome distraction. It seemed that I might actually have a chance at some semblance of a normal life.

And for about a month, I did.

Then, one afternoon, I walked into the parking lot to find a man yelling into a megaphone. "Ask Kylie what her real name is," his voice boomed out over the campus. "Ask her who Alisa Kaplan is. Ask her why she had to change her name. Ask her why she had to change schools."

The cat was out of the proverbial bag. News of the rape case spread like wildfire at my new school. Rumors about my promiscuity began anew. I started hearing the whispers in the hallways: "Slut." "Gold digger." "Pool cue." My new friends felt confused and betrayed by the fact that I'd lied to them. How could I have neglected to mention something this huge? And using a fake name—how creepy was that?

I couldn't explain how desperate I'd been to get away

from being defined by the worst thing that had ever happened to me. Most of my new friends backed away.

But I'd learned my lesson over the summer, and there was no way I was going back to being so lonely. This led to me making an important discovery. True friends are rare, but party buddies? They're everywhere you look. It may not be easy to find someone to listen, to support you, or to hug you while you cry, but you can pretty much always find someone to get wasted with. So that's what I did.

That year, my junior year of high school, was when I started drinking for real. I found that if I had a couple of beers in me, I stopped obsessing about what had happened to me. I stopped flinching whenever I saw a pool table or heard the pop of a Snapple bottle opening. If I had enough vodka in me, I didn't think about what it would be like to confront Seth and Jared and Brian from the stand, or to answer questions about the most intimate details of my brand-new sex life in front of a room full of strangers.

As my drinking got more and more serious, I came to rely on how effectively booze could blot out every shameful, guilty, frightened feeling I couldn't get away from any other way. "I don't want to feel like this, God," I wrote one night. "I'm not supposed to be the one in all this pain." I was right: It wasn't fair. But it wasn't avoidable, either—except when I was drinking, and then I didn't feel anything at all.

I started dating a guy called Mack, who was quite a bit older than I was. My parents disapproved, and my dad was so effectively scary that Mack was very respectful of me.

But I didn't need a boyfriend as much as I needed someone with an ID who could easily get me booze. Mack was more than happy to do that for me, leaving quarts of vodka hidden in the shrubs outside my parents' house so that I had a ready supply when I needed it.

Lying to my parents became second nature. It wasn't all that hard, to be honest. I took shameless advantage of the fact that they were preoccupied to the point of being overwhelmed with the legal proceedings. They spent hours every day on the case—driving me to therapy, talking to our lawyer, filling out all the paperwork required.

But I was also skating by on my reputation. Because I had always been such a good kid, my parents weren't primed to catch me being bad. It probably didn't even occur to them to worry about me sneaking out or smuggling booze into the house. Maybe I seemed a little distant, a little out of sorts, but that was only to be expected, under the circumstances. So all my troubling behavior slipped right under the radar.

I drank every day, all day. The quantities shock me now. Most of that year, I was drilling a quart of vodka a day. There are pictures of me, taken by my party buddies, of me driving drunk to school, my eyes barely open. There are pictures of us doing shots in the school parking lot at seven o'clock in the morning. Drug dogs patrolled the lockers at our school and would come into the classroom to sniff our backpacks, so I had to find a way around them; halfway through the school year, I could no longer get through the day without a drink. So I'd fill water bottles with straight vodka and hide them in the bushes on the school grounds.

Some days—the bad days, usually ones when my family was scheduled to meet with the district attorney's office, or had a deposition, or got news of some new violation of our privacy—I would have only one aim in my sight: to get so drunk that I blacked out. The prodigious energy and laser-like focus I'd once brought to my schoolwork and to making sure my color guard team knew their routines down cold? All of that was now single-mindedly trained on getting enough liquor to stay as messed up as possible. And, like everything else I'd ever set my mind to, I succeeded.

Lots of kids drank in high school, but I wasn't having a couple of shots at a party or some beers in the parking lot after a game. My friends were drinking to have fun, to get loose, to relax. But I wasn't out for fun; I was desperate. I was drinking the way a serious alcoholic drinks, the same way I'd been sleeping: to reach oblivion.

Every alcoholic and drug addict can tell you that oblivion gets harder and harder to find. In order to catch up with it, you need to keep upping the ante. That was why, in January of my junior year, I asked my friend Claire to help me get some cocaine.

I'd never done coke, but of course I'd heard of it. Everyone talked about how amazing it was and how great it made you feel, and I really wanted to believe that I could still feel great and amazing. Claire said her friend Ron could get some for me; she'd hook us up. But Ron didn't sell coke. What he sold was meth.

A week later, I was sitting in my Mustang in a restaurant parking lot with Ron. I'd brought another friend for moral support, and I could hear her swift intake of breath as he racked out some lines on the case of a CD on the center console of my car.

Now, I didn't know much, but I'd seen enough movies to know that coke is supposed to be powdery. This stuff wasn't powder—it looked like a smashed diamond, with big shards in it.

I spoke up. "What is that? Is that crack? I thought you had coke."

He shook his head and said, "I'm giving you something a thousand times better than coke, trust me. This will do more for you than you could ever imagine."

I was so hungrily chasing stupefaction that I didn't even ask again what it was. It was my friend in the backseat who asked the follow-up question. "Seriously, what is that?"

He laughed and said, "Are you kidding? You don't know? It's meth."

At that, my more sensible friend in the backseat shook her head: She was out. Meth was hardcore. Everybody knew how insanely addictive it was and how crazy it made you. She had no intention of turning into one of the tweakers you'd see on the news, with their sunken faces and their messed-up teeth and the sores they picked into their own skin.

But all I'd heard was the part about meth being a thousand times better than coke, and that was enough to intrigue me. So when Ron rolled up a dollar bill and passed it to me, I leaned over the center console—and blew.

I'd never done a line before, and I guess I got confused, because instead of sucking it up into my nostrils, I exhaled. Meth went everywhere! Ron got incredibly angry at me. At first, he was trying to clean it up off the floor, but I was clear with him: I was not going to do a line that he'd scraped out of the carpet on the floor of my car. (Little did I know I'd eventually get there.) Still irritated with me, he laid out another line. This time it worked.

Tears started pouring out of my right eye. I sat bolt upright, in a belated panic. Had Ron poisoned me? I turned to him and started yelling. "It hurts! It hurts! Is it supposed to be burning like this?" It burned so badly, I thought something must be wrong.

But Ron was laughing at me again.

"Yeah, that's normal. Just lay your seat back and be quiet."

I did what Ron told me and laid my seat back. The car was quiet as the meth dripped from the back of my nose into my throat. It is the most putrid, disgusting taste you can imagine, and yet it was a taste I would come to crave, to fantasize about, to love more than my family or myself.

A few minutes later, the drug hit my bloodstream. Ron had been right. This was the feeling I'd been chasing. I'd never felt so alert in my life, so attuned to everything around me. It was as if I'd been given a superpower: I could do anything, conquer anything. That disgusting taste was the gateway to the single best feeling I'd ever had, and I couldn't wait to taste it again. And again, and again, and again, and again. Before we were out of that parking lot, I was negotiating with Ron for my next line.

My friend in the backseat was starting to freak out, so we took her home. On the way, I called my friend Claire, the one who'd introduced me to Ron.

"I think I just fell in love," I told her.

Claire then confessed that she'd been doing meth for a couple of months, and we spent the rest of the drive talking about the drug like a couple of lovelorn teenagers. Which, in a way, we were.

And then I went back to Ron's apartment and stayed up doing meth with him for the next three days.

Meth was the ticket I had been looking for out of my misery. Weed and booze, I could see, had been mere child's play. Meth was even better than sleep.

Needless to say, it didn't take me long to discover firsthand that methamphetamine is one of the most addictive substances on earth. Here's why: Meth dramatically increases the release of a chemical in the brain called dopamine. Dopamine is the "reward" neurotransmitter, released every time you do something that gives you pleasure or satisfaction. You get a little hit of dopamine every time you move up a level in Candy Crush, for instance, or nibble on a piece of chocolate.

But doing meth dumps a huge amount of dopamine into your brain—like you've eaten the best piece of chocolate in the world, multiplied by a million. As soon as it hits you, you get an intense, euphoric rush, and then you don't want to eat, or go to sleep, or do anything besides the drug.

Unfortunately, experiencing that massive dopamine dump over and over has a devastating effect on your brain. The first of those effects is that the receptors in the brain that allow you to feel the rush become less sensitive, so you need more and more of the drug to get the good feeling. That decreasing sensitivity also means that you get less pleasure from everything else.

Not surprisingly, over the long term, meth use is highly destructive. It aggressively suppresses appetite, so users experience weight loss and often severe malnutrition. Tooth grinding is common, which is why so many addicts get meth mouth: rotten, broken stumps where healthy teeth used to be. Speed bumps are the sores and scars you see on meth users' arms and legs. Many people have tactile hallucinations, most commonly the feeling that bugs are crawling all over them or under their skin. Scratching to the point of causing self-injury is common, and the meth user's body can't mend its own tissues as well as it should, so the sores take longer to heal.

Meth gives you all of this, plus paranoia, irritability, anxiety, aggression, and often violence, not to mention all the lying, cheating, and stealing you're doing in order to get your next fix. Most disturbingly, studies have shown that using meth over a long period actually changes how the brain works. Meth users have difficulty learning and recalling information for years after they've quit. This may explain why people addicted to this drug develop such serious emotional and intellectual problems, many of which persist long after the person has stopped using—which is tremendously difficult to do, by the way.

Not a pretty picture, right? But even if I'd understood what was in store, it wouldn't have stopped me. You know the tremendous relief you feel when you finally twist the knob on the stereo after your music has been on too loud for too long? How the whole world suddenly feels calmer and more manageable? That was how doing meth made me feel, like I could finally claim a moment's peace and quiet by turning the volume down on all the sick, sad, frightening feelings that would otherwise plague me every waking moment of every single day.

I'd been asking Him for answers, but after I found meth, I gave up talking to God. I wrote my brother a letter, telling him I understood why he was an atheist. In my journal I wrote, "It's pretty harsh, but at this time in my life, this is how I'm feeling. *I do not believe in God.* It's hard for me to say that, but as of right now, I have given up."

I can't tell you how much I hate seeing those words in my own handwriting, or how much I hate to own up to them here. I hadn't had a very deep relationship with God or a very complete understanding of how He was working in my life. All I knew was that, despite my prayers, He hadn't made me feel better or delivered me to oblivion.

Meth, on the other hand, never failed me. After about six months, I had stopped snorting the drug and started freebasing, which is when you smoke the drug off a piece of aluminum foil. When you smoke meth, you get higher a lot faster than after snorting it. As soon as the smoke hits your lungs, you start feeling it, and that was what I wanted: to feel it right away.

Freebasing hurts. The chemicals in the foil cause painful blisters on your tongue and on the back of your throat. I converted a marijuana bong so that I could smoke meth out of it, and carried it everywhere with me. I named my bong, as if it were my pet. That's how into it I was.

I could function on meth and still not feel anything. I barely remember my junior year at all. I was constantly drunk or high. I look at pictures from that time, and they might as well be photographs of a stranger. I don't remember most of my friends' names, or a single family dinner my mom made, or anything I learned at school. I certainly wasn't doing the important work that might have helped me down the road, like processing the violation of the trauma I'd endured or girding myself to testify.

Looking back on it, I can remember how terribly lonely I felt. It's ironic, because loneliness was one of the feelings I was so desperate to avoid. It's almost a physical memory, like pain. You know when you're watching a horror movie, and you almost can't stop yourself from screaming at the screen: "No! Don't go in there!" That's how I feel when I remember that time. The choices I made then meant that I lost a big chunk of my life. I know why I did it, of course. But I wish I'd known what I know now, which is that I did not have to walk through the valley of the shadow of darkness by myself. There was someone right there with me, the whole time. All I had to do in order to feel His love was open myself up to the realization that I wasn't alone.

But I didn't know. I had found the oblivion I'd been searching for, and I couldn't see anything else.

## CHAPTER FIVE

# *Hung Out to Dry*

F or most high school students, senior year means applying to colleges and going to prom. I spent my
senior year in rehab, before testifying at my own rape trial.

We had expected that Seth's dad would hire the best and
the most expensive lawyer for the guys. But nobody was
expecting an eleven-person defense team.

One of the lawyers they hired was a former state
Supreme Court justice. Another was infamous for his ability to get jurors to ignore video evidence. He'd done it for
the cop who'd been filmed beating Rodney King and for
another police officer who'd been accused of excessive force
with video evidence. He'd developed an almost magical
reputation: How could you sit there and watch an unarmed
man being brutally beaten, long past the point of submis-
sion, and then vote not to convict the men who'd beaten
him? It felt almost supernatural, as if he could get jurors to
disbelieve their own eyes.

The lawyers were only the beginning. The private investigators, we discovered, were part of a larger team, headed by a retired FBI agent. The defense hired a consultant from the O.J. Simpson trial to help them select the jurors they believed would be most sympathetic. They hired an audiovisual expert, who was charged with coming up with different, multicolored ways to present evidence to the jury, as well as a publicist.

These were very big guns. When my parents saw the resources that the defense was throwing at the case, they began to feel deeply alarmed.

And yet, as everyone kept reminding us, we had the videotape. I hadn't seen it, of course, and neither had my parents. But we could tell it was bad. A thirty-year veteran of the police force choked up when he was talking about it with my dad. Everyone who had seen the video always said the same thing, in the same horrified tone of voice: that the DA could probably just play it for the jury and go home. Even then, I was more cynical. *If only it were that easy,* I thought.

Nobody was consulting me on anything. I went to the appointments my parents made with the lawyers, but only because I had to be there. Nobody spoke to me or asked my opinion; most of the time, I sat in the corner and played solitaire on my phone while the grown-ups talked over my head. A couple of times, they even sent me and my mom to do some shopping at the mall.

My age had a lot to do with it; as a minor, my parents had to speak for me. But there was another dynamic at work, too. My dad felt a tremendous amount of guilt and shame because he had not been able to protect me, and he responded to those feelings in the aftermath of the rape by becoming overly protective. If he had anything to do with it, nobody would ever hurt me again. So he did everything he could to shield me from further unpleasantness—which often meant speaking for me and intimidating our own lawyers so they wouldn't ask me questions that would make me uncomfortable.

Everything I knew about the case, I knew from eavesdropping at those meetings, piecing together the bits and pieces of information I could gather. That feeling of powerlessness threatened to overwhelm me, the feeling that I had unwittingly set into motion a cascade of dominoes that were set to topple everyone's life. All I had to do was look around me to see the damage I'd caused. What kind of a person would do something like this to her friends? No wonder I had no one left. I had brought this upon myself, I felt, and all I could do was stand there, watching in horror as the effects rippled out to hurt everyone else in my life.

Serious trial preparation began, and I watched my parents aging right in front of my eyes. The lines on my dad's face seemed so deep they might as well have been etched in stone. More disturbingly, my mom started experiencing numbness in her face and tongue, making it extremely difficult for her to speak and eat. Her doctors said it was a reaction to the overwhelming stress. One day that summer, I realized with a start that I could see her scalp shining through in spots, where hanks of her beautiful golden-blond hair had fallen out—another stress reaction, and more evidence of what I'd done to their lives.

My parents never stopped loving and supporting me, but I wasn't a fool: I could see the tremendous strain they were under, and I knew I was to blame. For a while, their marriage was even in jeopardy. Their twenty-eight-year rock-solid relationship was on the rocks, and it was all because of me.

On top of the emotional and financial burden, participating in the trial required a seemingly endless amount of time and work. My parents often stayed up late into the night dealing with the case. We were drowning in paperwork, and it often seemed as if my mom did nothing but drive me to and from therapy and appointments with the lawyers. As the pressure increased, my parents fought more and more, and my brother withdrew. He didn't blame me for the rape, but it was hard for him not to resent me for the turmoil and the chaos in our household when I was at the center of it.

To me, the message was clear: I wasn't just worthless, but actively destructive.

The preparation for the trial terrified me. Of course I knew that my history would come to light. My party girl phase had been a very short, stupid period, but I'd managed to cram a lot of pretty big mistakes into those six months. Preparing for the trial, I came to understand that every single one of them was going to be trotted out for the jury. Now, the law is clear: Rape is a crime, no matter what someone's behavior has been in the past. But that's not how it works in the real world, and it soon became clear that the defense would move heaven and earth so that everyone would learn what a slutty liar I had been.

Meth was my only escape from the swirl of feelings that threatened to overwhelm me, and I clung to it like it was a life preserver. But in September 2003, the first week of my senior year, my parents discovered what I was up to.

They'd had their suspicions that partying was going on, of course, but they thought I was drinking—maybe smoking pot. This was shocking enough for them, because I'd always been such a good girl. So they'd responded the only way they knew how, by locking me in. I'd always had their trust before, because I'd earned it. Now I had none. My parents drove me to school and they picked me up. I wasn't allowed out on the weekends, and I wasn't allowed to be home alone. Where once they'd been trying to protect me from the guys lurking outside, now they were trying to protect me from myself.

But you can't outwit a drug addict. If getting high was my job, then I was Employee of the Month. Locking me in didn't work. I developed ever more elaborate schemes for sneaking out of the house after they were in bed. For instance, I'd leave my pajamas outside on the porch, so that I could change back into them before heading back into my room. If my parents caught me, I could pretend I'd gotten up to get a drink of water.

One night, my parents busted me, drunk. My mom had woken up in the middle of the night to use the bathroom and checked the house alarm. Of course, it was off because I'd turned it off in order to sneak out, but my mom thought she'd forgotten to set it, and turned it back on.

So I rolled back into the house at about five a.m., so drunk that I couldn't stand on my own two feet; I had to crawl on all fours to get up the driveway. The alarm went off, scaring everybody half to death, myself included. My dad charged down the hallway, gun drawn, alarms going off all around us. He found me drunk out of my skull, trying to change back into PJs as fast as I could. Unfortunately, I was so wasted that I'd ended up with both feet stuck through one leg of my pajama bottoms.

My parents didn't see the humor in the situation. Instantly, they put me into an outpatient program for teenagers with substance abuse problems.

I didn't even break stride. I was Employee of the Month, remember? It was the easiest thing in the world for me to cheat the program.

My parents are into vintage cars. It's their main hobby. They buy them inexpensively, fix them up, show them off, and then sell them. They spend a lot of time at car shows; in fact, their whole social circle and most of the charity work that they do revolves around their cars. One night, my brother told them he had plans and wouldn't be home to keep an eye on me. My mom had finally gotten her dream car, a cobalt-blue and white 1955 Chevy Bel Air, and she was taking it out to a car show—which meant that I was going with them.

Of course, I wasn't going anywhere without getting high first. So I locked the bathroom door, did a line, unlocked and opened the bathroom door, and turned—a bag of meth in the other hand—to wipe down the countertop. That was when my mom walked by.

She couldn't see what was in my hand, but she knew it wasn't right. She followed me into my room. I was trying to be super-slick, so I pretended to be straightening my bed covers while I was actually sliding the bag of meth under the pillow on my bed. I thought I'd gotten away with it for a second—but then my mom sent me to the car so she could be alone in my room, and I knew I hadn't. But then she came out and got into the car and didn't say anything.

I will never forget that drive. I was sitting in the backseat of the Bel Air, sweating bullets. I was pretty sure that my mom had found the drugs. But if she had, why wasn't she saying anything to my dad?

After a virtual lifetime's worth of stony silence, we got to our first stop: my dad's automobile repair shop. My mom and dad went inside. And when my father came out of there, shaking the baggie of meth, he was as angry as I had ever seen him in my entire life. He looked to be on the verge of a heart attack. By then, I was too high to care. With every word out of his mouth and shake of his finger, I rolled my eyes, a big smirk on my face.

Truth was, my dad had no idea what was in the bag. When he had been a cop, crack was the big drug. Meth was more marginal, a hard drug that crazy bikers did, and it was usually blue.

My mom started crying: "Tell us what it is." I finally

admitted that it was meth, but I told them it was only my third or fourth time doing it, instead of the truth, which was that I'd been using heavily for more than half the year.

When they heard it was meth, my parents instantly became terrified that I was overdosing right in front of them. We got back into the car so they could rush me straight to the emergency room.

At the ER, I fought like a cat, spitting and hissing and shouting every curse word I could think of. My parents were wide-eyed with disbelief and horror: Who was this lunatic? I had transformed into someone they'd never seen before, someone they didn't know.

Four of them had to hold me down, but the nurses finally got some blood. When the doctor came back with the results from my blood test, he looked deeply alarmed. He asked me how long I'd been using. I repeated the same lie I'd told my parents: *Just a couple of weeks, I swear.*

The doctor looked at me hard, and then he asked me again—more clearly, as if I didn't speak English, or hadn't heard him correctly the first time around.

At that point, I knew I was busted. And for a moment, I didn't care. I almost wanted my parents to find out. If they knew I was addicted to meth, maybe they'd understand how much pain I was in. In that moment, I really wanted them to know.

I looked at the doctor. "Seven months."

I could hear my mom break into sobs behind me. Shock radiated off my dad.

The doctor looked down again at my chart and nodded. "That sounds about right. You using every day?"

I said, "Yes. Usually at least twice."

That's how my parents found out that I was addicted to methamphetamine. They knew I'd been drinking heavily, and they probably suspected that I'd used other drugs as well. But they'd never suspected anything so serious. I had been addicted to methamphetamine for seven months, and they'd had no idea.

The next day, they sent me to an inpatient rehab, and I got clean. The withdrawal was the worst pain I'd ever been in. I thought I'd go crazy. I was so lethargic and depressed that simply brushing my teeth would wear me out. And of course, as soon as the drug was out of my bloodstream, I found myself face-to-face with everything I'd spent the last year and a half trying to block out of my mind. The shame and humiliation and powerlessness and pain rushed back in to fill the space where the meth had been.

I hated my parents with a rage that blinded me to everything else, and I wouldn't let them come visit me in rehab. As far as I was concerned, I'd had one crutch that had actually worked—meth—and they'd knocked it out from underneath me, leaving me with nothing at all to lean on.

They never abandoned me, though. Here's part of a letter my dad sent me when I was there:

When the going gets tough, your friends get going— in different directions, that is. But your family comes running to your side, with love and support. So lean on us, let us be your pillar. We will hold you up and support you until you can build enough faith in yourself to support yourself. The dictionary describes faith as "A confident belief in the truth, value, or trustworthiness of a person." You must also have faith in us, your parents. Faith in knowing we can, will, and want to help you put your life back together again. Please put faith in our many years of experience and knowledge. Put faith in our love for you. And if you should fall back again, have faith in knowing we will be there to pick you up, brush you off, and start again, as we have done many times in your life.

*SO YOU HAVE FAITH, ALISA!!* Faith in your parents, for together we can fight this thing with lots of work, love, and support.

My mom was completely amazing after I was discharged. She was so proud of me, and made it clear that she'd do anything she could to help me stay clean. For instance, one day she went to Michaels and bought every single craft item she could think of to keep my hands busy. That fall, I made tons of jewelry for gifts and lots of little pieces of decorative stained glass. I found that I could get absorbed in making a tiny beautiful thing, and I enjoyed it.

Ultimately, though, the pressure was too much. I hadn't done the work I would need to do for rehab to work; I didn't have anything real or substantial to fill the hole I'd tried to cram full of drugs. So when I went to a Christmas party, December 2003, not quite four months after my release, I hooked up again with someone I used to use with. Within a week, I was using heavily again.

$A$s preparations continued, it became clear to everyone that the district attorney's office would be no match for the million-dollar team that Seth's dad put together for their defense. Our team was well-intentioned, and they were working as hard as they could. But I was a mouse, and Seth's dad was coming at me with an elephant gun.

Before the trial began, the defense hired a focus group to try out various strategies, and they quickly arrived at a strategy they were sure would succeed: They would highlight my previous missteps and destroy my credibility. They knew that the jury would be appalled and disgusted by what they saw on that tape—anyone in their right minds would be.

Their solution?

To make it seem as if I'd engineered the whole thing.

Much has been written about the way the legal system revictimizes victims. But I had absolutely no idea how horrifying the experience would be. Activists often say that rape is the only crime where the victim is put on trial. I call it reraping and say, completely without irony, that the actual incident had nothing on my experience at the trials—at least I was unconscious for the rape.

I wasn't in the courtroom for the opening statement, but reporter Scott Moxley was. Here's what he wrote about it in the *OC Weekly*: "In just his opening statement, a pacing, finger-pointing [defense attorney] told the jury that the girl—next to the tape itself, the prosecution's star witness—is 'a nut,' 'a pathological liar,' 'a cheater,' an 'out-of-control girl,' 'the aggressor,' a wanna-be 'porn star,' 'a troubled young lady,' 'a tease—that's what she is!' 'a mess,' a 'master manipulator,' a 'little opportunist,' 'a compulsive liar,' 'a cheat—that's what she is' and a 'callous' drug addict and alcoholic who trimmed her pubic hair, bragged about liking group sex and once drank a beer in a car."

According to the defense, I was a pathological liar and a whore who had consented to group sex as well as to being videotaped. I had feigned unconsciousness in order to further my dreams of becoming a porn star. I had even had consensual sex the night before the rape. Never mind that in the video you could see the boys signal to each other that I'm passed out. Never mind that I didn't flinch when they hit, slapped, and pinched me, or when I urinated on myself after they shoved a pool cue into my vagina. Never mind that I vomited before passing back out. Never mind that I was sixteen years old.

Riding home, we'd hear snippets from the trial reported on the radio. I'd felt for more than a year like I'd had no control, but this was a higher order of helplessness. It felt like what it was: psychological warfare.

The only bright light was my victim's advocate for the trial, Shirley. Gentle but plainspoken, Shirley was a proud grandmother who had nonetheless seen some of the very worst things humankind had to offer. She'd guided hundreds of sexual assault survivors through the legal system, and I couldn't have asked for anyone better to hold my hand. Over time, she became a mentor, a second mother, and a best friend to me.

During the trial, Shirley was with me every step of the way, telling me how strong I was, and how brave. She told me how much my willingness to testify meant for other women and girls, especially all of those women and girls who couldn't testify. She told me that enduring this trial was the hardest thing I'd ever do, and that surviving it meant I could survive anything. But of course, she couldn't protect me from the viciousness that surrounded me everywhere I went; nobody could. There was nothing anyone could do to stop the onslaught.

I testified at the first trial for four days.

The defense pulled no punches. Every time I walked into the courtroom, they petitioned to have Shirley removed. I didn't want my parents or other family members there to hear what the defense was saying about me, so Shirley was my only support. Luckily, the judge allowed her to stay, although they did prevent me from holding the smooth, oval crystal she'd given me to hold in the palm of my hand. This beautiful, clear stone was the talisman that Shirley gave to all of her clients when they were on the stand. "You are so, so strong," she'd say. "Pour all of your strength into that stone, so that the girl or boy who comes after you can borrow your strength." What that meant, too, was that we could draw on the strength of every survivor who had come before us. Thanks to the defense, even that was a comfort denied to me.

Each time I got up onto the stand, it was as if I were being attacked by a pack of wild dogs. The defense's lawyers would get up in my face, screaming, the spit flying out of their mouths and onto my face. They said things about me that were so disgusting, I couldn't stop myself from gasping, as if someone had crashed their fist into my guts. On a number of occasions, I cried so hard I couldn't speak.

But the biggest problem for our side was that I couldn't testify with conviction. There was a simple reason for that: I didn't remember anything. The only thing I clearly remembered from that night after Jared gave me the drink was about thirty seconds of it, when I came out of my stupor just long enough to throw up. All I remembered was seeing my bare legs and knowing that I'd gotten vomit in my hair. After that, everything is blank again.

So when I was asked on the stand about that night, all I could do was tell the truth. "I don't know." Or, "I can't remember."

I didn't know then how commonly rape victims are accused of seeming cold or unfeeling on the stand. I was barely keeping it together up there; if I'd let myself feel any emotion at all while I was testifying, I would have fallen completely to pieces.

It was also deeply unsettling not to know what had happened to me. I knew the bare outlines, of course, like everyone else in California. But there was still some part of me that didn't completely believe it, a tiny part of my mind that refused to accept that my friends had really done what everyone said they had.

There was a way for me to know exactly what had happened, of course: by watching the video. But I wasn't allowed to see it. My parents were already concerned about the clearly destructive effects that the trial was having on me, and they honestly thought seeing the tape would break me. "We had to protect you. We thought you'd commit suicide," my mother said later. "In the best-case scenario, we thought seeing it would drive you crazy, that you'd end up in an institution."

They may have been right, but their decision meant that I had only the most shadowy understanding of what had happened to me on that July night. Plus, I was consumed by guilt. I couldn't believe that what had happened to me was as bad as everyone had said it was—bad enough to justify everything we were all going through, and everything we were putting my former friends through. At some level, I held myself accountable for setting into motion the events that would hijack not only my own life, but also the lives of everyone in my family, as well as the men who'd hurt me. It was more than I could handle.

A very common response to a victim expressing guilt is: "Are you crazy? You were unconscious! No matter how you were dressed or how promiscuous you were, nobody deserves to be sexually abused with a pool cue." You won't get any argument from me on that front. But for the duration of the period where I was using drugs and not infrequently since then, I have often asked myself, *What did I do to deserve it? What did I do to make it happen?*

I understand now that survivors often feel guilt because we want to feel control. I was powerless the night I was raped—literally, passed out and passed around. And complete powerlessness is a truly terrible feeling. A feeling of guilt, however twisted that might be, allowed me to feel a little more in control of what had happened. But it sure didn't help my emotional state at the time.

Not surprisingly, as the trial progressed, so did my drug use. My parents were completely frantic. They were beginning to understand how serious my drug problem was. They loved me, and their memories of the goofy, sweet, straight-A student I'd been blinded them to what I'd become. My mom bought me clothes and made my favorite foods. They did everything in their power to help me, but their life preservers couldn't reach me. Nothing could.

Every day of the defense's testimony was more outrageous than the one before. Even now, knowing about victim blaming, I am astonished by some of the things that happened in that courtroom. I heard an adult man tell a room full of strangers that I loved to give blow jobs and have sex doggy-style. A porn star was called in to testify that, in her expert opinion, I had only been pretending to be passed out. A medical expert came from New York to tell the jury that actual consent wasn't required because it wouldn't have been possible to put a pool cue into my anus unless I consciously relaxed those muscles, never mind that I was unconscious and possibly drugged. The defense played the tape of my medical exam, over and over. My private medical records were leaked to reporters without our consent.

The most shocking development was when the lead defense lawyer told the jury that, in his opinion, I should have been charged with raping Seth, Jared, and Brian.

I don't make excuses, but I can tell you that I drank and did drugs so that I could stop feeling the shame of hearing grown men smear me in terms so extreme that they were talking about a person I didn't know. I drank and did drugs so I could stop seeing the hunted, sick look on my father's face when he thought I wasn't looking, so I could stop feeling the shame associated with ruining so many lives, including the lives of the men who had attacked me. So I could forget, for just one minute, that I had to spend every waking minute trapped in a body that had been degraded and abused in unspeakable ways, and then thrown away.

I didn't know then that those aren't feelings that go away, that they're feelings I'd have to live with forever. I didn't know then that I would be working through and praying on those feelings for the rest of my life. Actually, I'm glad I didn't. Because if that knowledge had come without knowing that I'd have God to keep me company on that journey, then there's no question at all in my mind that I would not be here today. I would have made sure of that. In fact, I very nearly did.

Between rehab and the media scrutiny, school had become completely untenable for me. I was homeschooled for the last two months of my senior year so that I could graduate with the rest of my class.

My mom got what she wanted: She did see me cross the stage in a gown and mortarboard. But it was hardly the day she'd dreamed about. I was so drunk, I could barely make it across the stage. My parents were scared for me, and scared of me. There isn't a single photograph of my graduation day.

Less than a week after I graduated high school, the defense rested.

California law was clear: A person can't have sexual relations with another person who is incapable of giving consent. The jury had seen the video, which showed me so clearly unconscious that the experienced police deputies who first saw it believed that they were watching an act of necrophilia. They'd seen my so-called friends give a thumbs-up and then a "go-ahead" gesture, to indicate that I was indeed passed out. They'd seen me urinate on myself without otherwise moving when Jared shoved the pool cue so deeply inside me that it hit my bladder—and then seen my attackers high-five each other, squealing with disgust and laughter.

Still, the jurors remained unconvinced: They couldn't

agree that Seth, Brian, and Jared had had sex with me without my consent. My prior behavior implied consent, they claimed, and anyway, I hadn't shown enough emotion on the stand. After three and a half days, they were still deadlocked. Because a unanimous vote is required for a conviction, the judge declared a mistrial.

June 28, 2004, almost two years after they'd attacked me, my assailants walked out of the courtroom, scot-free.

The juror who had held out to hang the jury gave an interview, reeling from what had happened. "I can't believe they saw the same video I did," she kept saying.

She was another hero, another Good Samaritan, like the woman who turned in the tape. She must have been under a lot of pressure in that closed room, and she could have simply thrown in the towel, rolled over so she could go home to her life. But she didn't. She believed me, and she fought for me, and I would have a lot of cause to think about that over the years.

Unfortunately, her bravery didn't make the difference that day. My mom was on the phone with Shirley when we heard the news. Beaten down after months of humiliation, I was devastated but not completely surprised. My mom wept, but I didn't have any tears left. Instead, I screamed. And screamed, and screamed, and screamed.

Later, I remembered thinking: *Wow. You really can buy anything.*

# CHAPTER SIX

## *It Leaves a Hole*

T he jury's verdict left me completely bereft. I'd gone through months of shame and humiliation for nothing. I no longer cared whether I lived or died.

Not everyone was reeling from the injustice I felt. In July, a grand jury reported the results of its investigation into actions by officials in the sheriff's department for allegedly suppressing information that Seth and two friends had been caught with marijuana in their car in 2003 (while Seth was out on bail), but they determined there was not enough evidence to prove those officials had violated criminal law. Also that month, Seth was arrested on misdemeanor charges of statutory rape after allegations that he'd had sex with yet another sixteen-year-old.

About a week after the declaration of a mistrial, Chuck Middleton, chief assistant district attorney, the DA's second in command, called and asked for a meeting. He wanted to talk to me about retrying the case.

Chuck seemed kind and almost grandfatherly—an impression that evaporated as soon as he began to speak about what the guys had done. This case was clearly a passion project for him. So much so, in fact, that although he'd stopped trying cases, he came back to retry mine. But first, he wanted to make sure that I was on board.

"If I reopen this, will you testify?" he asked.

He knew I didn't have a choice. Still, he asked, and it was the first time anyone had consulted me on practically anything since I'd been raped. It was such a relief to be treated like a person with opinions and thoughts, as anything other than a dumb, slutty, sad-sack teenaged victim. Chuck made me feel that I had something of value to contribute. He made me feel like I was part of a team, and it truly meant the world to me.

They couldn't have found a better prosecutor. Chuck was incredibly experienced in the courtroom, with particular expertise in sexual assault. I'd seen evidence of that experience without realizing it when he'd made it a special point to establish a connection with me. He didn't need my cooperation, particularly—if he'd called me to the stand, I would have had to testify, whether I wanted to or not. But Chuck understood how essential it is to make the victim feel she has a voice.

He simplified the charges so that they'd be easier for the jury to understand. The biggest change from the first trial was that we were no longer trying to prove that the guys had drugged me. I thought they had, the cops thought they had, and everything I remembered from that night and experienced the next day was consistent with the use of a date rape drug. But there wasn't enough physical evidence to prove it. Instead, Chuck would focus on proving that I had been unconscious, and they'd had sex with me anyway, no matter how I'd gotten that way.

Most importantly, Chuck was the right person to help the jury over what everyone now understood was the biggest hurdle, at least as the defense had chosen to handle the case, which was my past. Here was a clearly decent, honest, upstanding man (and the father of two teenagers at the time) asking the members of the jury not to be swayed by the bad choices I'd made. Regardless of my history, he would tell them, I did not deserve what had happened to me. As he would say at the trial, it's about "what they did, not who she is."

As I write this, I get angry all over again. Should my history have mattered? Does any woman—anyone?— "deserve" to be raped? Of course not. But in the eyes of that first jury, my history had mattered. To win, we had to make sure that it didn't matter to the second one.

I agreed to testify. But as soon as I did, I began to regret it. At least at the first trial, I hadn't known what to expect. I'd walked in there as a lamb to slaughter. The second time around, I knew better. I woke up bathed in sweat from nightmares about taking the stand in front of a roomful of strangers and hearing those grown men scream the most disgusting things they could think of at me while I cowered in shame and fear. Plus, our family was still being followed and stalked, and it hadn't gotten any less frightening. I was using drugs every day, a couple of times a day, and drinking, too. Still, there was hardly enough meth in California to dull my dread.

In September 2004, I met a guy called Neil. He was gorgeous—a former football and wrestling star. He'd parlayed his rock-star status in high school into becoming one of the most powerful drug dealers in town. He was also physically abusive to his girlfriends, as I would discover when we got together. But his business meant that we always had drugs, and that meant we were pretty much always high. It also meant a complete immersion in the drug world: shady characters coming out of the woodwork, and frequent trips to the disgusting places they lived in. It also meant trouble with the law, and I was arrested for the first time in October 2004.

Being in high school had kept me together somewhat. I was a complete druggie mess, especially in my senior year, but at least I'd been functional. After I graduated, whatever remaining sense of responsibility I might have had evaporated. There was no reason not to stay up for four days straight, doing meth and then whatever obsessive chore caught my fancy. My parents' pool had never been so clean.

Without school, there was no reason to shower, to change my clothes, to brush my hair or do my nails. It might sound shallow, but all the little ways that we groom and take care of ourselves signal to other people, to ourselves, and to God that we value ourselves. Letting myself fall into complete and total disrepair was the outward representation of my belief that I wasn't worth anything at all, not the time it would have taken to run a file over my nails.

After a couple of months with Neil, I wasn't just using, but had started to deal. My weight dropped precipitously to just over a hundred pounds on my five-seven frame, but I was no supermodel. My face got the hard, gaunt, sunken look of a habitual meth user, with the telltale giant black bags under my eyes. But the worst part was the sores.

Meth addicts are notoriously obsessive when they're high; they can't leave things alone. I was obsessive to begin with, which made meth the absolute worst drug for me. As many addicts do, I picked at my own skin. At the beginning, that meant I had a welter of unhealed scabs all over my arms and legs, and I pulled my own hair out, leaving bald spots where there should have been healthy hair.

But as my addiction got worse, I turned my attention to my face. I would sit in front of a mirror for hours, sometimes for days. I plucked all of my eyebrows out. During one binge, I worried away at my pores so relentlessly that when I was done, my entire face was nothing but a giant, raw layer of flayed skin. There's no other way to say it: I basically peeled my own face off. I can still feel the pain, and the shock of stepping back and seeing my whole face in the mirror for the first time.

The defense intensified their smear tactics. The newsmagazine *48 Hours* did a piece on the case. We participated, but it was a terrible mistake and turned out to be another smear piece. To begin with, the segment was called

"Eye of the Beholder," which implied that different versions of the truth applied, depending on who you were talking to. Much was made of Seth's "good, old-fashioned values." I particularly enjoyed the shots of him doing his homework around the kitchen table with his dad.

Meanwhile, my former friends were interviewed about my "flirtatiousness" and promiscuity. My hesitation to participate in the interview because of my trust issues was made to sound like paranoia and defensiveness. The piece mentioned my drug use and arrests, while remaining wistful about Seth's "poor judgment" and concerns about his future. Is that what it's called when you sexually abuse someone with a Snapple bottle? "Poor judgment"?

In October 2004, Seth got into a car accident. The post-accident Breathalyzer revealed that he'd been drinking, and his bail was revoked.

As for me, I had the drugs. Some days, meth was the only thing I could count on. After a while, my parents delivered an ultimatum: I could only stay at home if I was clean. So I did what someone who is completely desperate not to feel anything would do: I moved in with my abusive, drug-dealing boyfriend, Neil.


I was getting high with Neil when my cell phone rang. Chuck Middleton was in the middle of intense preparations for the second trial, and there was a question he had to ask me. Even in my drugged-out state, I could hear that there was compassion in his voice when he spoke.

"Alisa, I'm sorry to do this to you. But we think you need to watch the video."

The first jury had complained that I had appeared cold and unfeeling. Chuck felt that I'd seemed unemotional in part because I still didn't know what had happened to me, except the barest outlines.

Of course he was right. If I had been conscious for what happened to me—if the guys had had to pin me down and restrain me by force, if I'd been able to fight back, if I'd been conscious for what they did—I would have a completely different relationship with the incident. The terror and humiliation and powerlessness I had felt would have come across clearly to a jury, and I would have had much less difficulty convincing them to feel what I had felt.

But I had been completely unconscious, and I hadn't felt any of those things. That flatness and lack of affect had hurt my ability to convey to the jury what a horrifying effect the rape had had on me. The only way to get over that hurdle was for me to come face-to-face with what had happened that night. And Chuck knew, as sick as it must have made him to ask, that the only way I'd ever know would be to watch the video.

My parents were vehemently opposed to the idea of me seeing it. They were furious at me for considering it and livid with Chuck for suggesting it. (Neither of them have ever watched it.) The case had taken an unreasonably long time to come to trial (I once heard a law professor call this tactic, which is often used in sexual assault cases, "victory by delay"), so I was eighteen by that point—an adult.

My parents couldn't legally prevent me from seeing the video. But they did not support the decision, and they refused to go with me to see it, in the hope that I would reconsider. I didn't, of course.

Late afternoon on January 28, 2005, the police came to pick me up at Neil's house. They would take me to the police station where I would watch the video. In preparation, I got as high as I possibly could.

Shirley was there to support me, along with another investigator, but they turned their backs to the screen to give me some privacy. Then I sat there and watched as all the shadowy details I'd been struggling for three years to reconcile resolved on the screen in front of me into cold, hard facts.

I'd said over and over again that I wanted to know, but as soon as my brain could make sense of the images on the screen, I knew I'd been wrong. The truth was much, much worse than anything I could have imagined. Finally, I understood the way all those cops had looked at me, and that last juror's outrage. About ten minutes into the viewing, I realized that the inside of my mouth was so dry I couldn't swallow—my jaw had been hanging open in shock and disgust. But I didn't know how to stop the video, or where in the police station to go for water, and I couldn't get it together enough to ask for help. So I stayed where I was, my mouth gummy and parched, and watched.

The video is twenty-one minutes long, although the assault took longer than that; we'll never learn what happened when the taping was paused. When it begins, Seth is trying to pull my shirt up. I push his hands away and say, "No." My words are badly slurred, and I'm slumped over, barely able to sit up. I say, "Seth, I feel ill." Then, thirty seconds later, I slur, "I'm so [expletive] up."

Those are the last words you hear me say.

Loud rap music plays as the boys ham it up for the camera, laughing, dancing, smoking cigarettes. Seth screams, "Put it down for the militia, [expletive]!" There I am, naked, first on the couch, then on the pool table. I don't move. The three of them drag me around, have intercourse with me, slap and pinch me. At one point they drop me so hard you can hear the thudding sound of my head hitting the floor. I don't react at all. Then they penetrate me vaginally and anally with a Snapple bottle, a juice can, a lit cigarette, and the thick end of a pool cue. I never move, or even flinch.

Twenty-one minutes is a long, long time. I didn't watch all of the tape. I never moved from my seat, but the television was set up in front of a window and the sun was going down outside—a real Southern California sunset, a riot of glorious pinks and oranges and blues. Every once in a while, I'd give myself a break by taking my eyes off the screen and looking out over the top of the television, to where the sun was going down.

For instance, the part where Seth and Brian are pressing down on the outside of my abdomen, so that they can feel where the pool cue is inside me, through my belly, until they hit my bladder and I urinate all over myself—I didn't watch that part, but let my gaze drift out to the horizon, where the giant, fiery sun was making its descent.

Susan Schroeder was the chief of staff at the District Attorney's office. She was another amazing ally on our team, the most ferocious tiger you could possibly want in your corner. Susan has seen some truly terrible stuff over the course of her career (including the video of my rape), and she made a comment that stuck with me.

She said, "Seeing something like that video is like pulling a nail out of a piece of wood. It leaves a hole."

She was right—not only about the video, but about the whole experience. My happy childhood and the love of my parents had given me a sturdy scaffolding. But in the middle, where solid footing should have been—my self-esteem, ordinary development, my hopes and dreams and goals for the future—there was nothing, a gigantic emptiness. Always, there was the threat that I'd lose my balance and fall right in to the engulfing blackness, never to be seen again. I threw everything I could think of into the hole to plug it up: I did drugs and alcohol, and hopped from bad boyfriend to worse. But I didn't know that the chasm itself wouldn't go anywhere until I found something of true substance to fill it.

My parents had been right: Seeing the video took a tremendous toll. I was already in pretty bad shape, but that afternoon at the police station nearly broke me. It became clear that the drugs would be how I lived and died, and, frankly, that was fine with me.

The constant access to drugs meant that my connection to reality became more and more tenuous. I stayed up on one binge that lasted thirteen days. Neil's mom had raked the leaves in the yard, and when I opened the door, I saw the pile of swirling leaves turn into twenty snarling, slavering Doberman pinschers, snarling and attacking the door. I was losing my mind.

My old friend Beka got in touch with me around then. She wanted to apologize for deserting me and to find out how I was doing. Of course, all I wanted to do was to get high. "Come out with me," I wheedled. Misery loves company; maybe I'd feel less bad about the drugs I was doing if I could get Beka to do them with me. Maybe she'd even pay for them.

Once it became clear to her how far gone I was, she once again told me that she couldn't talk to me or see me. "You're not Alisa anymore," she told me, and I could hear the tears. "I don't want to be around you high. I don't want to be around meth, period. Call me if you ever clean up."


When you get clean, you make amends for the things you did when you were high. But there isn't any way to easily make amends for the things you do when you're a drug addict. I lied, I cheated, I stole. I sold drugs to kids; I got my friends addicted and then lied and cheated and stole from them. I will spend the rest of my life coming to terms with the things I did during those years. And while I do feel that my drug use was a response to the rape and its aftermath, I take full responsibility for everything I did in those years when I was on drugs. I have to.

Shirley, my victim's advocate, could see exactly what was happening. She was furious with me, but she didn't withdraw. "I'm not giving up on you. Better than anyone, I know your potential," she told me. It meant a great deal that she never stopped fighting for me—even when the person she was fighting was me.

One day, she took a stand. My parents and I had been called down for an appointment at the district attorney's office. I was living with Neil, and I remember making them wait outside for me in the car for a long time because I wasn't high enough to leave the house yet.

We met first in Shirley's office. Shirley is petite with a pretty face, surprisingly spiked short white hair, and loving, compassionate eyes. She's the best listener I've ever met; she looks deep into your very soul to make you feel she has all the time in the world to hear and understand and appreciate what you're saying, and I had never met anyone so quick with a hug.

When she has to defend one of her victims, though, the Mama Bear side of her comes out. Suddenly, she's clipped, professional, and no-nonsense—completely unafraid to take it to the mat and willing to fight to the death to protect her client. I'd only seen that side of her with others, though, so it was a little shocking to me to see how coldly she was looking at me that day in her office.

94

My long blond hair had always been my pride and joy. I had always made sure it was clean and shiny—neatly trimmed, blow-dried, and well brushed. Before I started doing meth, I was the kind of person whose shoes and eyeshadows matched her bag, and most days, I'd choose a piece of jewelry that picked up the colors in both.

It had been a long time since I'd cared about any of that, and it showed.

Shirley's experienced gaze took in my stringy, greasy hair and my broken, filthy fingernails. I became uncomfortably aware of the way the stained clothes I was wearing hung off my body.

"Did you take that coat out of the trash?" she finally said.

I bristled. What kind of a thing was that to say to someone? But the truth was, I didn't have the slightest idea where I'd gotten the grimy red coat I was wearing.

Coldness radiated off Shirley as she went with us to the meeting at the DA's office, where I alternated between apathy and belligerence. My own lawyer screamed at me, telling me I was sabotaging my own case. He was right, of course, but I didn't care. Afterward, Shirley asked my parents if we wanted to go have lunch. My parents said yes, and I said no. What did I want with food? All that eating and talking was a waste of time, getting in the way of the only thing I passionately wanted to do, which was to get high again.

Shirley said, "Fine. No lunch. But you're not going home. You're coming with me." Her mouth set in a tight, hard, line, she sent my parents back to their car. "Turn the radio on and get comfortable," she told them. "We might be a while."

It was a cold, gray, rainy day, but Shirley didn't seem to notice the weather as she marched me down the street. A couple of blocks away from the courthouse where the DA's office is, there's a Skid Row populated by drug addicts and the homeless. That's where Shirley took me.

I was raised in a nice middle-class suburb; I'd never seen anything like this. There was filth and trash everywhere. Graffiti covered the walls. Newspapers and wrappers and food debris were scattered all over the sidewalks, and we stepped over piles of excrement, at least some of which was human. The smell shocked me.

Figures wearing rags hunched together against the cold and rain. Others slept on collapsed cardboard boxes, their possessions in the ratty plastic bags under their heads. Some of the people we passed looked up, their eyes dull and life-less, but many of them were too far gone to notice that we were there. I leapt straight up into the air when a giant pile of garbage piled up against a building rolled over, startling me. It wasn't trash at all, as I had thought, but a person.

Shirley's face was grim as she said, "You better look around and get used to what you see, because this is where you're going to land if you don't get clean. You see these people? If you're not careful, you're going to end up living down here."

As alarming as I found the scene, I had no intention of revealing my revulsion to Shirley. I rolled my eyes at her.

"Do me a favor and spare me the Scared Straight crap, okay?"

"Fine," Shirley said, pointing to one guy in particularly bad shape, passed out near a puddle of vomit. "That guy? You're going to be his girlfriend."

At that, I snapped. "Look at these people! Look how horrible they look. They look like bums. I don't look like a bum. I look like I have a place to live, because I do."

Shirley shouted right back, "No, you don't. You might have a place to live, but you still look like trash. You're disgusting. You think you look better than these people, but the truth is that you'd fit right in down here."

I hadn't had the best attitude about our little excursion from the beginning. But when Shirley told me I looked homeless, I got extremely defensive. I probably hadn't taken a proper shower in a few days, but the idea that I looked like a street person made me completely furious. (Shirley must have known that my vanity was the best way to get through to me.) It was a testament of how tremendous my sense of denial was that I could not see any connection between those poor people and myself. There's always a line that a drug addict thinks she'll never cross.

I turned my back on Shirley and started to march back to where my parents were waiting in the car. Before we got there, though, she caught up with me, put her hand on my shoulder, and spun me around.

"Alisa, honey," she said, with tears in her eyes. "You're such a smart, beautiful girl. I know this has been hard, and you didn't ask for a bit of it, but you've got everything in the world to live for. I'm begging you to let me help you. Why are you doing this to yourself?"

I told her the truth, my words so sharp I hoped they'd cut her. "Because I like the way the meth makes me feel."

For the first time in months, I'd told someone the truth. Except maybe it wasn't the complete truth after all. The real answer was that I liked doing meth because it made me feel like I didn't have any feelings at all.

Shirley let her hand drop from my shoulder and watched silently as I got back into my parents' car. I was so furious, I didn't even say goodbye.

On the drive back to Neil's house, I told my parents that I had no intention of ever speaking to Shirley again. "I want a new victim's advocate," I told them. My mother, who had become extremely close to Shirley and saw her almost as a sister, tried to make me see reason: "If Shirley didn't truly care about you on a personal level, would she bring you down here? This isn't her job. Whether you can see it or not, people do love and care about you. All we're trying to do is to keep you safe. We don't want you to end up like those people living on the street."

I told my parents what I'd told Shirley: that I knew what I was doing, that I'd never let it get so bad that I'd have to live down there, and that I could take care of myself. Then I refused to talk to them the rest of the way back to Neil's.

Shirley thought she'd wasted her time. I didn't have the courage to tell her how lonely and broken I felt. Whether she knew it or not, though, she had planted a seed in me.

Sometimes that's the best you can do. Even if you don't know when that seed will sprout—or if it will at all—planting a seed is always worth doing.

During the first trial, Shirley had introduced my mom to the concept of tough love, the idea that I'd never get clean while my parents were supporting me financially and otherwise. Still, for more than a year, my parents had kept coming and picking me up whenever I called. I'd tell them I wanted to get clean; I'd swear to it, outlining all the ways that this time would be different. Then I'd eat everything they had in the house, watch their cable, and sleep in my childhood room under freshly laundered, sweet-smelling sheets.

But when the cravings for drugs would get too intense, I'd head out again, back to Neil and the streets and the drugs—often without even saying goodbye.

Shirley is an incredibly compassionate person, but she's also had a lot of experience with drug and alcohol abuse because of her job. She could see, clear as day, that my mom making me lasagna exactly how I liked it and buying me clean cute T-shirts to replace my own soiled clothes wasn't helping me to quit the drugs.

It took Mom a long time to hear what Shirley was telling her. There was absolutely nothing hard about my Mom or about the way she loved people. My dad was the fierce one, the tough guy, the one who didn't take any flack from anyone. But my mom was the sweetest, most generous, most openhearted person anyone could ever hope to meet—and that was true whether you were her daughter, a stranger, or a guest in her home. Still, in the months before the second trial, she came to understand that her nurturing and love was hurting me, not helping.

One day, I called home with some nonsense junkie excuse. Someone had stolen my last five dollars. Could they come pick me up? My mom showed up, but the atmosphere in the car was tense. I was coming off a binge, irritated and anxious and, of course, pretending not to be an emaciated, scarred up, drug-sick lunatic, while my mother was pretending not to notice how filthy and thin and unwell I looked.

Then my mom noticed me scratching myself. She leaned over, looking closely, and we both saw little bugs leaping off my greasy, foul-smelling sweatshirt. I had fleas, like a neglected, unloved dog.

My mom pulled the car over, reached over me, and opened the passenger-side door.

"Get out," she said.

Something that day helped the message strike home. Maybe it was as simple as the world's tidiest person not wanting her pristine car to become infested with fleas—or finally understanding how far her daughter had gone, that I'd get into her beloved car crawling with them. Whatever it was, my mom had finally heard Shirley's tough love message, and she was done.

Shocked beyond belief, I got out of her car. A few days later, my dad told me that after years of letting me use her for money and food, my mother had disowned me. I was not allowed anywhere near their home, and she did not want to have any contact with me. In the future, when strangers asked her about her children, she would tell them only that she had a son.

It was as if my parents had completely reversed roles. When I was growing up, my dad was the disciplinarian, the one who laid down the law, and my mom was always the softie. But I'd pushed her too far. The message was clear: I'd have no relationship with my mother again until I got clean.

Neil's abuse intensified. He blackened my eyes, left bruises and cuts all over my body, knocked out one of my teeth, and fractured my arm. My dad drove me to the hospital, frantic to get me clean and away from him, but I wasn't going anywhere but back to drugs.

Neil and I were arrested on drug charges, and then arrested again. It was self-sabotage, pure and simple. I was wresting some control over my life, in the most self-destructive way possible. According to my twisted logic, if everything had to go down the toilet, at least I was the one doing the flushing.

After the second arrest, I realized I had nowhere to go. Neil was still in jail. I couldn't call my parents; my mom would make sure my dad didn't come to help. I went by the house of a couple I knew because Neil and I had sold them drugs. I spent two nights sleeping on their floor, at the foot of their baby's crib. We used drugs in that room, while the baby was right there. It was one of the most shameful things I remember doing, but I was too far gone for it to register.

When that couple kicked me out, I went to see if Neil's parents would let me stay at their house, but they only let me in long enough to fill a backpack with some of my stuff. So I went to find Sammy, another guy I knew from the drug world.

Sammy lived at home, but his mom was a nurse who worked the graveyard shift. He told me I could sleep in his room at night when she was at work, but he was so scared of her finding out—she was religious and incredibly strict—he made me sleep underneath his bed, staring up at the springs. There wasn't enough room under there for me to turn over so I could sleep on my side.

I begged Sammy to let me use the shower. It would be the first one I'd had since spending the night in jail. At first he said no way, but on the third night we got ridiculously high together, and I was able to wear him down until he relented.

The shower is where I was when Sammy's mom's came home unexpectedly.

Her shift at the hospital had been canceled. Twice my size and strong as a bull from lifting patients, she stormed right into the bathroom and yanked me out of there, soaking wet, naked, covered in soap and shampoo. She didn't want to let me rinse my hair, but I convinced her to give me some privacy to put my clothes on, and as soon as she stepped out, I locked the door behind her and jumped back in the shower to rinse off. She was so mad, I thought she was going to break the door down. I got dressed before she could rip it off its hinges, without drying myself off. As soon as I opened the bathroom door, she picked me up and threw me and my backpack out the door, into the freezing cold November night.

The whole time, she was preaching at me, throwing Bible verse after Bible verse at me to let me know that the trouble I was in wouldn't end in this lifetime. "You better find Jesus," she yelled, before slamming the door. "Even with all this that you're doing, God still loves you."

There I was, high and sopping wet and freezing, without anywhere to go. *There's no God,* I thought. *God wouldn't put me through this.*

A few weeks before, Neil and I had ducked into a Dumpster stall in an alley behind a McDonald's in a rundown shopping center to get high. We'd seen a busted couch sitting nearby. It was the filthiest thing I'd ever seen, so ragged and heavily stained that you couldn't tell what color it had been when it was new. Graying foam inserts leaked out of the few remaining cushions, and in a number of places the tattered upholstery had ripped off the frame, exposing the bare wood and springs underneath. It was such a depressing, disgusting piece of furniture that Neil had made a joke about it.

But it was two o'clock in the morning, and I was wet and freezing and high, with no money, no cell phone, and nowhere else to turn. So I went to find that couch.

The alley was terrifying. The only source of light was a tiny security light hanging over the Dumpster. Everything else was pitch black. "Anyone could be out there," I thought, and the idea made me so uncomfortable that I went into the Dumpster stall and squatted in there for a little bit, grateful for the shelter from the wind and the idea that at least I'd see someone coming. When I stopped feeling so high, I went back out to that vile couch. What I wanted was to fall asleep and to not wake up.

Half an hour before, of course, Sammy's mom had given me the answer. She'd served it up to me on a platter. God still loved me, she'd said. He loved me, as sick and screwed up as I was. There would never have been a better time for me to meet Jesus than in that alley. But I wasn't ready to hear.

Neil stayed in jail for ten days, and I spent the rest of them on that couch. Shirley had been right. I wasn't any better than those bums on Skid Row.

The biggest difference, in my opinion, between the first trial and the second was passion.

The defense had always had passion. As twisted and wrongheaded as it might have been, there was a deep conviction fueling their win-at-all-costs strategy. For the second trial, our side had passion, too.

Chuck truly believed that young men should not be permitted to do the things that those guys did to me— no matter what I'd drunk or worn, or whom I'd fooled around with. He believed that what had happened to me was wrong and that the guys who did it must be punished, or it would be sending a terrible message not only to them, but also to society at large.

I was high for the whole second trial, except for the days before I testified. In order to get me there, Chuck had my parents check me into a hotel, never letting me out of sight—all so he could guarantee I'd be clean on the stand. My mom was there, too. Although she had stopped supporting me as a drug addict, she never stopped supporting me as a victim.

Chuck ran the second trial very differently than the first one. The defense wanted to make sure that we didn't allude to the possibility that I'd been drugged. So Chuck agreed to a stipulation stating that the only substance in the cup Jared gave me was eight ounces of gin. They stepped into his trap. That stipulation opened a door: if that drink was the only drug I'd consumed (plus one beer and a hit of pot), then how on earth did I get so drunk that I passed out?

Chuck's experience benefited me in another way, too. During jury selection, both the defense and the prosecution get to pick the citizens they want to see on the jury. Each side has a certain number of choices they can reject. But how can you know who's going to be sympathetic toward your case? This is why picking juries is an art form.

The defense had hired a high-powered jury consultant, and some of the jurors from the previous trial acted as consultants, too. They were looking for certain kinds of people they thought would be most likely to relate to the defendants: people who hated law enforcement, people who wouldn't necessarily have a knee-jerk negative reaction to the idea of violence against women. They were also looking for people who'd be appalled and outraged by the idea of a woman with multiple sexual partners.

One of the potential jurors in our case was a Hispanic man, with tattoos covering his arms. His appearance, his ethnicity, and the fact that he lived in an area known for gang activity made the defense feel very comfortable with him. Plus, he didn't have a wife or any kids that he could imagine lying like a rag doll on that pool table. The defense was sure that the combination of all those factors would make him less likely to vote to convict.

But Chuck had thirty years of experience interviewing potential jurors for sexual assault cases. He'd interviewed this guy, and he'd listened to his answers. Maybe this guy did look kind of scary, but Chuck had found him to be quite sensitive and thoughtful, the kind of person Chuck thought would make a good dad someday. The defense practically fell off their chairs when Chuck didn't use one of his vetoes to get this guy off the jury. But they were probably more surprised when he turned out to be jury foreman.

I felt vindicated when I heard this story a couple of years after the trial. The defense had made a judgment about that juror based on his appearance. As it turned out, neither one of us would be so easily dismissed.

As the case went to trial, the defense approached us with the possibility of a plea bargain: The guys would serve time, but they wouldn't have to register as sex offenders. For me, that was an instant no. The sex offender classification was the most important thing for me. What they had done had left a hole in me. That night hadn't been youthful hijinks, boys being boys. It had been serious and damaging, with lasting effects. I wanted to make sure that what they'd done to me wasn't treated like some little mishap they could laugh off in the future or explain away with a wave of the hand to a future girlfriend. They had to own what they had done. If I had to wear my own scarlet letter, the placard around my neck that I felt everyone could see—THE SEXUALLY ABUSED WHORE—then they did, too. So I told Chuck that the only plea we'd entertain would be one in which they had to register.

The night before I was set to testify, my parents and I got a call from Chuck telling us that the guys were seriously thinking about taking a plea bargain—one that included agreeing to register as sex offenders. We were up half the night, hoping and praying that they would take it, because that would save me the horrendous experience of heading back into that courtroom. The very idea that I might not have to go back was like a stay of execution. Then, at the crack of dawn, we got a call telling us that they were fine with the jail time offered, but that they had once again refused to register as sex offenders.

I was devastated. I would have to testify again.

The next morning, I had a breakdown so severe that my parents thought I'd have to be hospitalized. It was in the parking lot of the DA's office. When I was testifying, we'd go from our hotel room to the DA's office, meet quickly with the team, and then they'd arrange transport for us to the courtroom. The press attention was so crazy that we had to be snuck into the courtroom through the judge's chambers.

I was fine when I got into the car—still a little shaky from lack of sleep, but feeling strong and sure of myself. And then a dreadful, creeping cold feeling came over me. Suddenly, I had a whole-body memory of how horrific it had been to sit in the witness box at the first trial. My throat closed as my mind raced, and my heart was beating so hard it hurt. I couldn't get a breath, and bright black spots appeared in front of my eyes.

I started crying and screaming. "I can't do this. I won't do this." I begged to be allowed to back out and started trying to claw my way out of the car.

By the time we arrived at the DA's office, I was a complete wreck, sobbing like a spineless blob of ectoplasm in the backseat. My mom tried to talk to me, but quickly realized there wasn't anything she could do to get me out of there, so she went up to the office and sent Shirley down.

I had locked myself in the car. Shirley waited patiently outside until I let her in, and then she crawled into the backseat with me. She held me and rocked me like a little girl. Silently, she let me cry and shake and rage. When she did speak, it was only to remind me why I had agreed to testify in the first place. "It's not only for you, Alisa, but so these guys don't think they can do this again to some other girl. Because I can promise you one thing: If they get away with it this time, they will do it again."

With my head in Shirley's lap, I allowed myself to be comforted. Once again, she knew precisely how to reach me. I wasn't strong enough to testify for myself. But thinking about all the other girls the guys might do this to—and more, all of the other girls all around the country and the world who would be vulnerable if we sent the message that what the guys had done to me was okay—made me feel braver. Thinking about all those other women was what got me out of the car and into the courtroom that day.

My fears, of course, had been totally justified. The defense made mincemeat out of me on the stand, attacking me so viciously it made it seem like they'd handled me gently at the first trial. Again, the case should have been very clear: It's against California law to have sex with someone who cannot consent throughout the act. But once again, it was as if I were the one on trial. For four days, the defense grilled me in the most humiliating way possible. Their goal was to convince the jury that I'd been awake—or that even if I was unconscious, I was such a whore that I would have consented to everything they did to me.

It was a horrible experience. I felt horrendously exposed and vulnerable, like they were ripping the skin right off me so that everyone in the room could stare at my insides. The humiliation was worse, now that I'd seen the video: I knew exactly what the jury was thinking when they looked at me, the images they had burned into their brains. And, after watching the video, I found myself even more powerfully disturbed by the tack the defense was taking. It was really shocking that those men could turn around and try to portray me as the perpetrator after seeing how limp and unresponsive I'd been.

Something else disturbed me. I was older and more experienced in the world during the second trial, and it felt to me like some of these older male lawyers were getting a truly unseemly amount of pleasure out of getting me to describe various sex acts. The sight of them leering at me as they asked their questions made my skin crawl.

But I made it. When they'd asked their questions at the first trial, I'd answered honestly: "I don't know." After seeing the video, I did know—more than I wanted to, in fact. So I could be very clear about what had happened, and about the emotional impact the rape had on me. I wept, openly and often, while I was testifying. Seeing the video had practically killed me, but no one could complain that I didn't show enough emotion on the stand.

And on March 23, 2005, a second jury convicted each of the three men of several counts of sexual penetration with a foreign object by intoxication. None of the men were convicted of rape or of assault with a deadly weapon. They would not be sentenced for another long year.

Years later, I asked Chuck Middleton why the guys hadn't been convicted of rape, and he explained that rape is specific in that it requires force (against the will of the victim) and penetration. One of the jurors in my case had held out on that charge.

This happens a lot. The good news is that there's a movement to broaden the definition of rape. In 2012, the FBI changed their definition of rape to "The penetration, no matter how slight, of the vagina or anus with any body part or object, or oral penetration by a sex organ of another person, without the consent of the victim."

That's more inclusive than the previous FBI definition, which was simply: "The carnal knowledge of a female forcibly and against her will." That definition didn't include male victims, rape with an object, or victims of forced anal or oral sex. And "forcible" could be used to exclude anything but overwhelming and potentially deadly violence, including crimes similar to mine, where the victim was under the influence of drugs and alcohol. Nobody had had to hold me down or use force, because I couldn't move.

The FBI's new definition is good news because it will dramatically change the way that these crimes are tracked and reported—and many people, myself included, believe that it will give a more accurate picture of rape in the United States. Unfortunately, local criminal codes seem to be heading in the opposite direction. Twenty-five states and the District of Columbia have stopped using the word *rape* in their criminal codes altogether. So a lot of real crimes aren't being counted when they should be. That's something I feel should change.

Not that it mattered to me then. When the conviction in my own trial came in, I barely registered the verdict. In fact, I was watching it on television, sitting on Neil's bed, high as a kite. Nearly three years of my life had culminated in this moment, but I didn't feel much of anything at all. It was over, and I didn't even call my family.

\*    \*    \*

Early in the spring of 2005, I met another drug dealer, Russell. He'd been attacked by a pit bull when he was younger and enjoyed a big payout from the settlement every year. Big money meant one thing to me: lots of drugs. Drugs were the only thing I was interested in. Then Neil beat me up worse than he ever had before. I broke up with him and moved in with Russell right after his check came through.

It was a frightening time, and not just because of the drugs. That summer, my parents' neighbor Bonnie, who looked enough like me to be my sister, was ambushed and brutally attacked outside of her house. At this point, the harassment of me and my family was so well known that Bonnie actually had the presence of mind to scream, "I'm not Alisa!"—at which point her assailant ran away. Her face was battered beyond recognition; multiple reconstructive surgeries later, the damage was still evident. I was completely terrified by what had happened to her and sick with guilt about it. The only thing that allowed me to forget were the drugs.

By June 2005, I was staying in a Motel 6, selling drugs, and attending the court-ordered rehab program I'd been sentenced to after I'd been arrested in the fall. I knew that failing a drug test would mean three and a half years of prison time, but I couldn't stop using.

Every Monday, we had a drug test. I'd used Sunday, and then drank two full gallons of water. (I'd even drunk hydrogen peroxide, because I had heard it could mask a positive result.) My urine was too diluted for a result, so my probation officer put me in a room for a few hours. When they tested me again, I tested clean.

She knew I was dirty. I knew I was dirty. Leaving, I could hardly meet her gaze, but she wouldn't let me off the hook. "Someone's giving you a second chance," she said, her eyes boring into me. I grabbed the discharge paper from her hands, ducked my head, and got out of there, on my way to getting high.

I wasn't ready. Still, her comment that day stayed with me, and a thought, however vague, penetrated my perpetual drug haze. The second trial had been successful. The second jury had believed me. We'd secured a conviction.

Maybe the idea of a second chance wasn't so crazy after all.

## CHAPTER SEVEN

# *A Way Out*

That summer, everything came to a head.

In March, Russell had gotten $32,000, part of his settlement from the dog bite case. By August, every cent of that money was gone. We'd spent it all—every last penny—on drugs.

I hadn't spoken to my mom in months, but my dad and I were still in contact all that summer. He was dedicated to keeping the lines of communication open. I think he hoped to show me that I was still loved and therefore still had a reason to live. I also think that staying in contact with me made my dad feel that he was still able to protect me in some way, though my condition was visibly deteriorating at a rapid rate. On the worst days, I think he was relieved simply to hear that I wasn't dead.

As he had been my whole life, my dad was my rock that summer. I wasn't allowed anywhere near my parents' house, but whenever I showed up at his shop, he would welcome me with love and open arms. He'd always find some little thing I could clean or file so I could make some money, though I'm sure he knew in his heart that I'd spend it on drugs as soon as I'd left him. Those afternoons with my dad were an oasis for me in the desert of my drug use. I'd talk to him for hours about the chaos and destruction of my life, and he'd listen and let me cry. He never judged me and he never got mad, and he never let me see how painful it must have been for him.

In July, I sent him a letter. In it, I wrote: "I'm not going to wait for these drugs to kill me." He recognized the letter for what it was: a suicide note.

I often wished during those days that I was strong enough—brave enough—to kill myself. Isn't that the worst thing? Every morning now, I am flooded with gratitude for so many things: my family and friends; my beautiful, sweet dog; the silly little bird that hops around my back lawn while I'm drinking my coffee after I've said my morning prayers. It's so sad, but it's true: That summer I hated myself for the fact that I couldn't step up and end my own life.

Russell didn't beat me like Neil had, but he was emotionally and verbally abusive. And when the money ran out, our situation became dire.

When Russell had first gotten the payout, we'd moved

into a relatively nice apartment. The idea was that we'd have more money for drugs if we stopped jumping from one sordid motel room to the next. But whatever effort we might have put into making the apartment liveable at the beginning got messed up pretty quickly. Buddies came over to get high and didn't leave. Then one of Russell's friends lost his own apartment, so he moved in with us, along with his wife and three kids. By July, there were ten people living there, on and off.

When the cash dried up, we stopped paying rent. The eviction notices started coming. One of the tweakers crashing with us took a Sharpie marker and graffitied filth all over the walls. We didn't pay our bills, so our electricity got cut off. That meant no air conditioning, even as the temperature climbed past 100 degrees. Nor was there any hot water for showers. Unless one of us stole a candy bar from the gas station for the kids, there wasn't a scrap of food in the house. Some nights I was so hungry I wanted to cry right along with them.

One afternoon in August, I showed up at my dad's shop to ask for gas money. We were so broke that I was running Russell's truck on fumes.

For the first time ever, my dad said no to me. He was done, he told me, with supporting a lifestyle that was going to kill me.

We got into a huge fight. I was furious, in part because I truly had planned to use the money for gas. So I screamed horrible, hateful things at him and gunned the engine. As I was about to screech off, my dad ran up to the passenger side of the truck and tossed a balled-up twenty-dollar bill through the window into the cab.

"Enjoy getting high on my hard-earned money," he told me, his face crumpled with hurt. "But that's it, do you hear me? That's the last time."

I drove away, hysterical. I'd lost my mom, and now I was about to lose my dad, too. And I knew that if he was done with me, I'd have no reason to live at all.

I went straight to a gas station and put the whole twenty into the gas tank. I got a receipt to prove it. I drove back to show it to my dad, but it wasn't the reconciliation I'd hoped it would be. Instead, he met me in the parking lot, and handed me a padded envelope. Inside was a framed photograph.

It was the last sober picture I'd taken with him, Thanksgiving of 2002. My aunt had taken it, and it was such a great shot that she printed and framed a copy for each of us. In the picture, I'm sitting on my dad's lap, my arm slung around his neck. I glow with health and happiness and promise, every hair in place, my smile wide and easy, my lip gloss perfectly touched up. My dad looks relaxed and incredibly proud, and he's wearing the very familiar teasing look on his face that means he's about to make a bad joke, probably at my expense.

You can tell, by looking at it, that these are two people who *get* each other.

My dad had kept the photo on his desk at work for years. It was the picture he'd show clients when he was bragging about me. Now, he'd put it in a padded envelope because he didn't want it anymore.

"I don't know where the girl in that picture is," he said to me before he turned away. "And I don't want to see that picture again until she's back."

It was a dark, dark moment, in a summer that had been filled with them. I drove away slowly. The thought came to me, unbidden, almost exasperated: *C'mon, Alisa. This isn't the life you're supposed to be living.*

The Holy Ghost was riding shotgun that day. That was the voice I heard, reminding me that I was loved and had a purpose on this earth.

A few nights later, I found myself alone in our filthy, roach-infested apartment. Russell and I were completely out of drugs, and I was desperate, so I got down on all fours so I could comb through the carpet for crumbs to smoke.

Suddenly, I started to weep as if my very heart was broken. It was like an out-of-body experience: I could see myself, as if from above, and what I saw shocked me. Where was the straight-A student I'd been, the Girl Scout, the captain of the color guard, the good girl with all her big dreams?

I found myself praying—or, more accurately, begging. "Please, God, help me. Help me, God. Please." I said it over and over again, crawling around our destroyed apartment on my hands and knees. "I don't know what to do, but I can't do this anymore. This is not who I am, or what I'm supposed to be doing. Please, God, help. I can't do it by myself. If I continue to control my own life, I'm going to die."

A couple of weeks later, on August 20, the police raided

the apartment where Russell and I were staying and arrested him on an outstanding auto theft warrant. They got ready to take me in, too.

The cop who was getting ready to arrest me looked at me with disgust. I was filthy, and living in squalor. My athletic body was practically wasted away, and my arms and legs and face were covered with open sores. By that point, I was no stranger to being treated like a pariah, but under his gaze, I felt sick with shame.

I begged for his mercy. I wanted to get clean, I swore. *Typical junkie crap,* I could practically hear him thinking while he was rifling through my purse. But then he found the list of drug rehab centers I'd been calling since that night I'd begged God for help.

He looked at me again. Thankfully, he could see that I was desperate for a way out of the life I'd been living, and he told me he'd give me a chance at one: the gift of a week. Over the course of the next seven days, he said, I could find a spot at a rehab or simply move along to another filthy drug house in a different town. But he promised he would come back to that house on August 27, and if I was there, he'd toss me in jail and throw away the key.

He gave me a second chance: "One week, you hear me? Seven days."

It was all I needed.

After they were gone, I took my meth bong, wrapped it in two black trash bags, and smashed the package with a hammer until I could no longer lift my arms to keep hitting it, pulverizing the glass into dust finer than grains of sand. Then, while Russell cooled his heels in jail, I went through detox by myself in the trashed apartment.

But as the clock ticked down on my gift week, I started to panic. I had spent the week clean, burning up the phone lines to every rehab on my list. Wait lists averaged nine months, and I knew I'd never stay clean without inpatient treatment. I also knew that if I started using again, it would only be a matter of time before I ended up dead.

But on the morning of August 27, exactly seven days after the cops had arrested Russell, my phone rang. Resigned to jail, with a week's shaky sobriety under my belt, I answered. A ninety-day inpatient rehab center half an hour away had an opening. The cost would be covered by my parents' insurance.

The opportunity I'd been praying for had been granted. This was the second chance I'd asked God for, and when it came, I grabbed it with both hands. My journey toward healing had begun.

No matter how bad my drug use got, every single day I would find a pay phone and place a collect call to my father, just to let him know that I was alive.

"Hi, Daddy," I'd say when he picked up.

I can't imagine now how either one of us tolerated those calls; the memory of them is so painful I can hardly bear it. For my dad's part, he says that, as horrible as they were, they were better than the alternative, which was not hearing from me at all.

The same thing that compelled me to make those phone calls helped me to stay clean in the first few days of rehab. I desperately wanted to stop using, but I had no idea how to do it, because I had no idea how to do it for me.

In my own eyes, I wasn't worth enough to stay clean for. I was a piece of garbage, a whore, a junkie. I'd made decisions—the months before I'd been raped, the night of the rape, and many, many nights afterward—that had led to my own life being ruined. I'd destroyed the lives of three guys, not to mention my own. My amazing parents had gone through untold amounts of financial hardship, stress, and straight-out harassment because of me. Their perfect, loving marriage had been badly strained. I had no friends. Those who hadn't abandoned and betrayed me, like Beka, had walked away when they'd seen what a colossal mess I'd made of myself in the aftermath of the trials. Once a straight-A student, the kind of kid who'd freak out over a B+ or a typo, I'd barely graduated high school.

I did have one thing going for me, though. Most of the people I met when I was using didn't have the solid upbringing I'd had. As far away as it seemed, I had a memory of the time before—before the rape, before the intimidation, before the humiliation and trauma of the trial. I had been happy as a child, though it had been a long time since I'd felt that way.

My father had told me that treatment in a serious inpatient program was the only way I'd get my mother back into my life. Though I'd put them through hell, I still loved my family deeply, and I knew how much they loved me. If I could get and stay clean, they'd let me back into the fold. The thought of being part of our family again was what kept me clean in those very early days. I may not have been worth anything in my own eyes, but I could get clean for them.

One of the very first things I did in rehab was set up the two framed copies of that picture of me and my dad on my dresser. It was nothing short of a miracle that I'd been able to hang on to both of them, but I had.

"How come you have two copies of the same picture?" everyone who came into my room wanted to know.

"When I leave here clean, I'll be able to give one of them back to its rightful owner," I'd say.

That picture meant something to me, too. Every morning, I would look at it, unable to reconcile the shiny, happy girl on my dad's lap with the lank-haired, hollow-eyed reflection that looked back at me from the mirror. That girl—that laughing, engaged perfectionist, a quip on her lips and every hair in place—where had she gone? Was she still in there, somewhere? How had I gotten from there to here? And was it even possible to get back?

You can get clean for someone else, as I'd gotten clean for my family. But you can't stay clean for someone else. You have to stay clean for yourself.

Helping with yard work was part of rehab. It didn't take me a lot of time watering the lawn to notice that the busted-looking house across the street from the rehab center had a lot of shady-looking visitors coming and going. A drug house! My heart sang. I headed back to my room, already cooking up a plan to sneak out, get some drugs, and bring them back in.

But as soon as I'd phrased it that way in my head, my plan went haywire. Why on earth would I bring drugs back to rehab? If I wanted to get high, why not just leave? I could remember all too well the time spent on those waiting lists, the frustration of not being able to get help when I thought I wanted it. Why wouldn't I at least give up the bed, leaving it available for someone who was in good faith trying to get clean?

Unbeknownst to me, my counselor, Tina, a former addict herself, had been watching me from the window while I was out in the yard. I wasn't the first resident to clock that drug house across the street, and Tina didn't need to be told what was going on. She showed up in my room about ten minutes after I came in and found me curled up in a ball in the empty bathtub, completely wracked with sobs.

But instead of rubbing my back and offering comfort, she asked me the same question I'd been asking myself: "If you want to score, why stay?"

She didn't mince words, though I was pretty near hysterical by that point.

"Nobody's keeping you here," she told me flatly, talking over the sound of my tears. "You're not on lockdown. You want to go across the street? Then go across the street. But if you go, understand this: You do that, you're never coming back." Then she turned on her heel and left the room.

I stayed in that empty bathtub for a long while. When I finally got out of there, I knew two things. The first was that I didn't want to die. The second was that I knew I would if I left. So I stayed in rehab.

That day was a turning point. For the first time in a long time, I had consciously chosen to live.

One of the pieces of advice that good therapists give trauma victims is to do things that will help them connect to the person they were before the trauma occurred. Before the rape and my drug abuse, I had been an athlete: a dancer and a runner. I had taken a lot of pride in how flexible and strong my body was. I had loved being fit enough to effortlessly knock out a seven- to ten-mile run before school. Obviously, my physical fitness had diminished significantly during the period where I was using drugs heavily. Not only had I horribly abused my body, but I'd become completely disconnected from it.

After that day in the bathtub, I started waking up a little early so I could spend an hour in the makeshift gym they'd set up in the rehab's basement. There were only a couple of machines, a dated treadmill, and some free weights, but that was more than I needed, and I began to work out.

I went, even on the mornings when I didn't feel like it. The routine kept me grounded. I started seeing muscles again in my calves and upper arms, which had wasted away to practically nothing. The planes of my thighs took on definition instead of hanging there. I did hundreds of crunches, allowing myself to get lost in the sweat and sensation. At night in bed, I could run my hand over my belly and feel the warmth that comes from muscles that have been vigorously used.

I started to remember how good it felt to be strong and fit, to be able to trust my body. My appetite, which had been practically nonexistent for years, returned. I was hungry, and food (even the food in rehab) tasted good. Within a few weeks, I had started to put on some badly needed weight. The face that looked back at me from the mirror was beginning to fill out.

Working out was a good first step toward getting healthy. But it wasn't until I started talking about the rape in rehab that my real recovery began.

I'd never discussed the rape in any depth before, and I was never the one to bring it up. The case had been national and international news, and I'd been outed in my own community, so everyone I came into contact with there knew my story. I'd been in counseling for a while, but my therapist had refused to continue seeing me when I couldn't stop using drugs. I had spent years talking to lawyers, of course, but not about my feelings. My boyfriends had been drug addicts, interested only in prurient details. In some kind of disgusting way, because the case had gotten so much attention, I was a little bit of a celebrity to them. What did I care if they were getting off on it, as long as they could give me some meth?

Human beings process a lot by talking about the things

that happen to them, and I hadn't really talked about anything. I didn't even keep a journal anymore. It was as if I
had completely lost my voice.

After a full month in rehab, you know the group of
women you're in there with at a level that's hard to com-
prehend in the real world. We'd shared and overshared, and
shared again. We knew things about each other that our
own mothers and lovers would never learn. Still, I hadn't
told anyone that I had been raped. When asked at the beginning, I'd told the group simply that I'd gotten into
drugs because I'd fallen in with the wrong crowd.

Then, about a month in, in line for dinner one night, I
tapped my counselor Tina's shoulder.

"You know that gang rape case that was in the news so
much, a couple years back? The girl on the pool table?"

She turned around to look at me, her big brown eyes
solid and calm, and nodded.

I took a deep breath. "That was me."

Tina knew already, of course. All of the counselors at the
rehab did; it had been part of my intake form. But I hadn't
said it out loud to anyone yet.

We filled our trays. Then Tina made a comment that
was so simple, and so true, it stopped me in my tracks. She
said, "That night is a big part of the reason you use. You
need to stop trying to run from that, so you can stop letting what those guys did to you ruin your life."

That was a revelation to me. For three years, what had
happened to me had been my identity. That was what I
was, wasn't I? A victim, a drug addict, the girl on the

news. The rape had been my own genesis story—the place where my new life, the terrible one, had begun.

But Tina was saying something different. She was telling me that those things didn't have to be who I was. I could choose my own identity, make my own life, choose a new beginning for myself.

It was a liberating concept, but it was also overwhelming. I sat with it for a while, but I was still so ashamed! A couple of days later, I expressed my frustration to Tina. I wanted a new life, a better one. But I felt stuck, like the women around me in rehab were progressing fast, while my own growth was stunted.

"Maybe it's because you haven't been completely honest yet," she suggested. "You're still ashamed of what happened to you. You've seen how powerful it can be to speak your truth; you see it every time you stand up and say out loud that you're a drug addict. Do you think that if you talked about what happened to you with the group, you might take some of the power back from your perpetrators? Could that be a way to get rid of some of this guilt and shame?"

It was a radical suggestion to eliminate the stigma of rape by facing it head-on. And so the next night, sitting on the floor in a circle as we always did for our evening meeting, I told the group about that July night and everything that had come after.

As I spoke, I kept my head down, tracing a pattern in the carpet with my finger because I didn't want to meet anyone's eyes. The room was completely silent except for my voice. When I finally looked up, every woman in the room was crying.

It was as if a huge boulder had been rolled off my chest. Tina had been right; talking about it had taken some of the power out of it. Everyone hugged me. They asked questions, and I found, to my surprise, that I had no problems whatsoever answering them. I was learning that there was a lot of support and comfort and empathy to be had out there, as long as I wasn't numb.

With the help of the other women in the group, I could see that the way I'd been using drugs had been a way of punishing myself for what I still felt had been my fault. As I started to get feedback from the group, I began to see that I owed sobriety to myself for the courage I'd shown in testifying. I owed it to my family for their unwavering support and love. I owed it to every victim of sexual assault who can't prosecute his or her assailant—and for every one who does, and then doesn't receive justice.

That night was a major breakthrough. But Tina was on guard, too, because she knew that once I started talking, I'd see that I'd never fully processed everything I'd lost. Clean, I could see the scope and breadth of what had happened to me. I'd lost the end of my childhood. I'd lost the person I'd been. There was a great deal to grieve before I could begin to heal.

## CHAPTER EIGHT

# Fake It Till You Make It

S obriety was frustrating. Some days, I'd take one step forward, only to fall two steps back the next.

I couldn't believe my progress wasn't faster, more linear. All I could feel was impatience. Why didn't I feel better? Why wasn't I recovered? Why wasn't I healed? I wasn't using drugs anymore. Hadn't that been the problem?

M y pastor likes to remind us that God's plans for us don't always coincide with the schedule we've set for ourselves. "Wait on God," he says, and the first time I heard it I felt goosebumps raise up on my arms. It's a truth I particularly need to be reminded of—so much so that I've written it on a piece of construction paper and taped it to the mirror above my dressing table. In my opinion, all of us could afford to meditate on the idea that God is always working in your life, although you and He may not be on the same schedule.

I sure could have used that reminder in rehab, though it wouldn't have meant anything to me yet. Because I wouldn't find true confidence in my sobriety until I'd taken a vital next step: developing a relationship with God.

I'd like to be able to tell you about my dramatic conversion moment. I wish I could tell you that, like Paul, I fell to the ground, blinded by the light. But there's an expression in AA: Fake it till you make it. And that's really how I began to become a Christian.

Once I got serious about getting clean, I looked around me and I saw one thing: The women who were successful at sobriety had some kind of spirituality in place. Not all of them were Christians, and not everybody called their higher power "God." But everyone in rehab who was making it work had turned their lives over to a power greater than they were. So I started doing what they did.

They prayed, so I prayed. At the beginning, I didn't have the slightest idea what I was doing. When I was younger, I'd had a sense of God, though I'd never prayed for anything more substantial than a good grade or for some cute boy to talk to me. Now that I was actively looking to have a relationship with Him, I couldn't feel anything at all. Praying often felt like I was talking to myself, like a crazy person on the street. *This is nuts,* I'd think self-consciously as I was doing it. Of course, as it always does, the prayer eventually started to work on me and in me. Gradually, I began to feel someone was listening.

\*   \*   \*

In the same way that I'd love to have a dramatic conversion story to tell you, I'd love to tell you that when I started to pray for real, I immediately felt the peace that comes from choosing to walk with God.

Unfortunately, that's not what happened. Instead, I got mad—really, really mad. Hopping mad. Livid. Enraged. Furious. So angry I could hardly think straight.

*Are you kidding me?* I thought. *"Let go and let God"? How could I trust Him? Why had He allowed this to happen to me?* I'd been a good person, for the most part. I didn't even litter! Okay, fine, the six months before the rape, I hadn't exactly been living the best life. But I'd been sixteen years old—just a kid, for crying out loud! I hadn't done anything that a lot of teenagers don't do, and I hadn't hurt anyone but myself.

Wow, was I mad. I was mad at breakfast, mad at lunch, and mad at dinner. I spent a lot of those early prayers yelling at Him in my head. *Where were you? Why didn't you protect me? How am I supposed to trust You now?*

Then, of course, I'd flip back to my default mode: feeling guilty. Surely turning my life over to a higher power didn't mean hollering and cursing at Him? I didn't understand the rules of this praying business. Was I compromising my sobriety? Was I going to Hell for thinking this stuff?

I didn't realize yet that God wants us to wrestle with Him. I hadn't yet read the story of Jeremiah, "the weeping prophet," who God sends to Judah to warn the people of the destruction that is coming because of their sinful natures. Jeremiah suffers terribly there and questions God (sometimes straight-out raging at Him), accusing Him of deceit and blaming Him for his loneliness and humiliation. God, of course, never stops loving Jeremiah. He is steadfast and consistent, no matter what. I'm pretty sure now that bringing our heartbreak and disappointments to Him in prayer is part of walking with Him. But back then, I was truly frightened by my prayer-time rants. Was I burning my only bridge?

When I told Tina I was questioning God, she nodded. She let me rail a little, and then she interrupted me. "It's fine to be mad—at yourself, at your parents, at the guys, at God—whoever it is that you need to be mad at. But you still gotta do the footwork, Alisa. Your recovery? It's on you. You have to work your steps, keep showing up."

Footwork was one of Tina's favorite things to harp on: How we couldn't expect to stay clean simply because we weren't using at that moment. Bad things happened to everyone, but nobody was to blame for the situation we were in. If we wanted to stay clean, each one of us would have to take responsibility for where we had ended up. "You gotta show up, do the work," she'd say, with a shrug and a shake of her head.

Her comment made me mad all over again, but of course she was right.

I thought of Tina recently when our pastor gave an entire sermon about "staying in." Too often, he said, we look for a way out when things get tough. But whether it's a marriage that's lost some of its spark, a pledge to a charity that's started to feel burdensome, or staying clean, we have to stay in.

It's not always easy. In fact, it can be incredibly, intensely difficult—as it was for Noah, for Moses, for David, for Job, for Paul. I believe that it's okay to turn to God and tell Him how hard it is, to show Him that we're struggling. But we can never forget that God has a plan for us, and that everything is happening the way it's supposed to be happening, and in His good time.

There's that "waiting on God" idea again. Wait on God, walk with God, wrestle with God, struggle with God. Just don't give up. No matter how hard the road gets, we have to remember that, and we have to stay in. I've come to see that Tina's "footwork" is another way of saying that you have to stay in. You have to do the work.

At some level, I knew my sobriety depended on this relationship I was growing with God, though I still didn't like Him much of the time. So though I didn't always feel like it, I kept doing the footwork: reading the Bible and praying. And sure enough, just as I was getting a little stronger physically with every workout, my faith also got a little stronger every day.

It had always been important for me to connect with something bigger than myself. As Shirley knew when she was holding me in the backseat of my parents' car before

133

the second trial, I could never have testified if I hadn't thought that what I was doing would make a difference for other women. I couldn't have gotten clean without knowing how important it would be to my parents. My growing relationship with God put all those experiences into context and allowed me to feel that my connection to something bigger was real and permanent.

There would be a lot of comfort for me in that, as soon as I was ready to receive it.

I've said that I take responsibility for all of the terrible things I did when I was addicted to drugs, but it took a while to get there.

Alcoholics Anonymous (and Narcotics Anonymous, its sister organization) is a twelve-step program. The fourth step requires the addict to "make a searching and fearless moral inventory of ourselves." And this fourth step has to be done with someone else. It's not enough to sit in a room and quietly think about all the terrible stuff you've done in your life as an addict. You have to tell someone else.

I can't tell you how much fear this step triggered in me. I'd been anesthetized when I was doing all those terrible things, but the good girl I had been wasn't so distant. When I was clean, thinking about everything I'd done made me feel sick to my core. I had to come to terms with all the disgusting things I'd done, to name them and own them, with no thick padding of drugs to protect me from

the feelings? And then I had to come clean and tell someone else what I'd done? No way.

As it was, there were some days where I felt I'd drown
in my own guilt. I couldn't see how wallowing around in
all the horrible things I'd done was going to help, and so I
procrastinated the fourth step as long as I could.

Tina, however, was relentless. I'd written a phrase from
group therapy at the top of the first page of my notebook,
and she made me read it over and over: "I am responsible
for a part in every relationship I've ever had, and I've
played a part in whether that relationship succeeded or
failed." I must have read that sentence a hundred times,
until one night those words revealed themselves to me.

I felt hugely guilty. But feeling guilty wasn't the same
thing as taking responsibility. In fact, feeling guilty wasn't
doing anything. It wasn't helping me to heal, or making
it possible for me to have a better relationship with my
family, or motivating me to stay clean. It certainly wasn't
helping all the people I'd hurt. Feeling the tremendous
weight of all that guilt made me feel like I was doing
something when I wasn't really doing a thing. It was just
another feeling I had to numb with drugs.

For a split second, I could imagine what my life would
feel like if I could let go of all the resentment and hate I felt
toward myself. It was as if the clouds had parted, and for a
single moment I could see a better life: how much happier
I'd be, how much more I'd be able to give to others. It was
then that I began to understand the fourth step.

What if I could take responsibility for everything I'd

done? Could I then stop feeling guilty, and maybe even start forgiving myself?

The possibility was tantalizing. I took a deep breath and sat down to my fearless moral inventory.

I ended up writing all night. I filled the entire notebook. Paging through what I'd written as the sun came up was totally devastating. There were more than a hundred names on my list of people I had hurt: 112, to be exact. I handed the notebook to Tina before breakfast, and then buried my face in my hands.

I met with my sponsor, Melissa, the next day—in a Starbucks, of all the places to do a fearless moral inventory. I knew her from meetings. She had a lot of years sober, and she'd patiently tolerated my doubts and impatience during those early days, when I wasn't sure I was going to be able to stick with the program at all. I'd often call her four or five times a day.

At Starbucks, Melissa listened quietly and calmly as I went through all 112 people I'd hurt. When I was done, she held my hands and told me to make amends where I could. (I eventually did, but it took a couple of years.) Then she drove me back to rehab.

Once again, Tina had been right. Just as it had helped me to tell my story to the others in my group, taking inventory robbed my sins of their terrible power. I thought that detailing them would only confirm that I was the worst person on earth, but it actually gave me a tremendous amount of relief. I had looked at the ugliest, most selfish, venal parts of myself. Once I'd held myself accountable for what I'd done—

and, in as many cases as I could, actually apologized to the person I'd done them to—I could start to let them go.

A funny thing happened after I did my fourth step. At the beginning of my stay at rehab, I'd taken private pleasure in breaking some of their little rules. We weren't allowed to wear our house shoes outside in the yard, for instance, but I'd sneak out for a smoke in my slippers. Similarly, there was a rule that we had to be showered and dressed at breakfast. I'd shower, but then I'd put my pajamas right back on, daring someone to call me out on it.

After I did my inventory, I stopped breaking those rules. I can't explain it, except to say that the joy went out of it. I found that it felt good to be accountable, to take responsibility for myself and my actions.

As my graduation from rehab loomed, Tina started asking me about my victim impact statement.

The guys were set to be sentenced in March 2006. At the sentencing, I would be able to confront Seth, Brian, and Jared with what they had done to me. Ideally, this would provide me with some emotional closure. I'd also be able to explain to the court exactly how the crime had affected me before the judge decided their sentence.

Ways the crime had impacted me? I sure wasn't short on material. But as soon as I put pen to paper, I found myself freezing up. I couldn't write it. Not even a little of it. Finally, Tina told me that writing my statement was a condition of graduating from rehab.

"I can keep you here another month on a county bed," she told me. "I'm the one who signs your release, and I'm not signing anything to let you out of here until you read that statement to me."

She was bullying me, but once again she was right. It wasn't a great idea to have me out there on my own, brand-spanking-newly clean, and rehashing all the ways that being raped had screwed up my life. If I had to do that, Tina wanted me to do it in a safe, controlled space, where I was surrounded by clean and sober people and all the support I'd need to get through it.

On October 21, 2005, I got a day pass from rehab so that I could go to the DA's office to practice reading my victim impact statement.

Reading those words aloud had a devastating effect on me, so I took care of myself. The first person I called after we got out of there was my sponsor. And right after I read my statement, my parents drove me back to rehab.

I have a copy of that statement in front of me as I write this. At the time, I thought it was a document of healing, but it is crystal clear to me now how sad and broken and lonely I was. Reading it now breaks my heart; I have nothing but compassion for that girl. And that's truly what I was, even three years after the assault: a child.

I was released from rehab on my eighty-ninth day, right before Thanksgiving. And on Thanksgiving Day, 2005, I gave the photograph of the two of us back to my dad. He had tears in his eyes when he saw what I'd given him, but he also told me that he'd never lost hope that I would.

# CHAPTER NINE

## *A False Start*

I t's good that I'm stubborn and a fighter by nature, because I did not have an easy time in the years that followed.

On March 10, 2006, almost a year after they were convicted, and almost four years after the assault, Seth, Jared, and Brian were sentenced to six years in prison, with allowances for time served. Most importantly to me, the judge ruled that they'd have to register as sex offenders for the rest of their lives. They wouldn't be able to get away with doing this to another girl.

Judge Briseno expressed concern about the defendants' lack of remorse after the fact, and was outspoken in his opinion about their behavior during the crime itself. "Their intent was to degrade the victim," he said, and there was disgust in his voice.

That was good to hear. Still, it was a deeply bittersweet moment. The allowance for time served meant that the men who assaulted and hurt me would each do less than three years in prison if they served their full term. It also meant that they'd already served much of their sentence in the much-cushier county jail, as opposed to state prison.

My lawyers were disappointed by the length of the sentence. I was disappointed, too, until unbidden, the thought came to me: "That's not for me to judge. God will take care of this." It was the first time I'd truly been able to turn something over to Him.

It might not have been the justice I wanted, but unlike a lot of women, at least I'd gotten some.

As we walked out of the courtroom, Shirley put her arm around me and stroked my hair. She was disappointed about the sentencing, like everyone else. But as always, Shirley had her eye on a bigger prize.

"Look what else God has given you," she whispered.

She was right. By the sentencing, I was six months clean and living with my parents.

I had gotten a good job as a buyer's assistant at a trendy clothing company. I had started college. I had a community of women friends to go to meetings with when we weren't out shopping or at the movies. My mom was talking to me again, although our relationship was still slightly strained. My hair was washed, and there was polish on my nails.

A lot of the people who'd known me at the height of my drug use showed up for the sentencing. Tiare was there. Chuck Middleton was there, obviously, and so was Susan Schroeder. Every single one of them made a huge fuss about how healthy and strong I looked. It was then that I realized that most of the people who had worked on my case had taken it for granted that my drug use would eventually kill me.

It's funny what you don't allow yourself to see. For instance, it wasn't until I started writing this book that I came to understand how closely my drug use shadowed what happened to me: I started using drugs right after the rape and was clean—however newly—almost four years and two trials later, for the sentencing of the men who had assaulted me.

Shirley was right. No matter what sentence had been handed down, I was clean and healthy.

It was a beginning, but it wouldn't be enough.

In AA we say that someone is "sober without recovery," or a "dry drunk." Recovering drug addicts have a similar expression: "Getting clean is only the beginning." Any of those would have been a pretty good description of my condition after getting out of rehab. I was going to meetings and had a community of sober acquaintances, but I wasn't seeing a counselor or getting any kind of formal help. My emotions were completely out of control—that was clear, even to me. Still, I thought I was the only rape victim who felt the way I did.

After I got out of rehab, I found myself face-to-face with

everything I had spent so long pushing away. All the feelings I hadn't allowed myself to feel while I was using were right where I'd left them, three long years before. I hadn't done anywhere near the work I had to do to deal with the trauma of the assault and the trials. I had yet to grieve my lost adolescence and the woman that I might have been. But I didn't want to do any of that. So I turned once again to my old friend: sleep.

I should have been grateful for my sobriety, but all I could see was everything I was missing. I spent my twenty-first birthday at an AA meeting. A lot of people would say that's a success story. But at the time, it only served to highlight everything I felt I was missing. Everybody else got to go party in Vegas, and I was sitting in a dank church basement with a bunch of alcoholics and drug addicts, nursing a cup of cold coffee.

I'd fallen very far behind. While I'd been selling drugs and sleeping on a couch behind a McDonald's, my peers had been dating and making friends, sitting in classes, learning about themselves and the world. Women my age were starting their real lives: They were settling down with partners, moving into their own apartments, beginning to establish themselves in the careers they'd chosen. By contrast, I was living with my parents and taking freshman review courses, relearning how to be a normal person in the world.

Nor was I likely to catch up anytime soon. Like many rape victims, I had massive trust issues, which meant it was hard for me to make new friends, let alone to date. I had no idea what I wanted to study at college or what I wanted to do with my life. All those baby steps you take during those interim years of late adolescence—the internships and entry-level jobs, the late-night conversations with your friends where you try on different hopes and dreams for size—I hadn't done any of that. I didn't even have hobbies. My hobby had been meth.

My relationship with God was an early casualty. In rehab, there were lots of people to worship with. There was always a pop-up prayer group in a quiet corner of the garden or someone holding an impromptu Bible study session in the back of the TV room. Away from rehab, I didn't have any context for my relationship with God. (It didn't occur to me to find a church.) A few months into my sobriety, I stopped reading my Bible, and my prayers became less frequent.

Once again, Tina had been right: I hadn't done the footwork, and so my sobriety was on shaky ground.

My perpetrators had been sentenced, but the case was still in the news almost every day. The lead defense attorney for the first trial had his license to practice law suspended after getting caught making deals with local bail bond agents. Seth's dad was caught cheating on his taxes. He escaped jail time by wearing a wire to help officials catch the sheriff, once his friend, who was accused of using his office for personal gain and of trying to derail a grand jury investigation. (He was convicted of witness tampering and sentenced to sixty-six months in federal prison.)

We'd pulled at a string, and the whole weave was start-ing to unravel. It wasn't a huge surprise to learn that these people were involved in illegal or immoral affairs. But these were massive scandals in our area, and every article about it referenced my case.

So much for moving on.

Then, in 2007, I started seeing someone. His name was Allen. I'd known him for a long time. He was impressive. He was as stubborn as I was, but he was dedicating his ferocious work ethic to living a full and amazing life. He was putting himself through culinary school and working two jobs to support himself as well as his mom when she needed help. In his spare time, he cooked at a soup kitchen. Unlike pretty much everyone else I'd ever dated, Allen was a decent person, a seriously good person, working hard to do the right thing. I fell for him hard.

He was also young. Hanging out with him made me feel like a kid again. I longed for all the carefree years I'd missed, and during the two years I spent with Allen, I made an effort to recapture that feeling.

But the truth was that nothing in my life—including my relationship with Allen—was really working. At heart, I wasn't happy or peaceful.

In December 2008, I moved into my own condo-minium, a couple of miles away from the house I grew up in. It was an important step toward independence, but I was desperately lonely there. I'd gotten a new job, too, working as a medical assistant. I was okay at work as long as I was busy, but if it got slow, I crashed emotionally. It was a job, not a career, anyway. I didn't want to work in the medical field, although I couldn't settle on what I wanted to study at school.

My life looked good on paper. But if I was on the right path, then why did everything feel so empty?

My control issues spiraled. Rape is about control, not sex, and victims often struggle with a need to regain some of the control they feel was taken from them. This can lead to a lot of anxiety and some very unhealthy behaviors.

I was no exception. Any tiny change to a previously scheduled plan would send me into a complete frenzy. If I had plans to see a movie with my parents, and they told me on Wednesday that they wanted to do it Saturday night instead of Friday, I'd freak out. Not because I had plans on Saturday, but because our plans were set in my head for Friday. When I left home in the morning for work, I had to wait to make sure my garage door was completely closed. If I didn't, I'd find myself driving around the block to check it. On the few occasions I was able to calm my anxiety enough to go to work without checking, I'd spend the morning in a state of unbearable anxiety—and as soon as my lunch break started, I'd run to my car and drive home to make sure it was closed.

My employers loved me because I spent hours maniacally labeling every file and storage container in the office. Every insurance vendor, every different kind of patient form and chart had its own spot and its own label, so that a temp could sit down and immediately know where everything was. That kind of neurosis might have been great for my employers, but it was not so good for me. A form filed in the wrong place would send me into a spiral, and every three months, I'd stay late into the night, hours after everyone else had gone home to their families, cleaning and organizing the whole office.

At home, I set my clothes out every night for the next day. It's good to be organized and to plan ahead, right? But I would do it if I came home so tired I could barely stand. Running a 104-degree fever, I would stagger around my room to set out the next day's outfit, complete with jewelry and complementary eyeshadow colors. What if I couldn't? There was no such thing as "couldn't"—if I didn't do it, I didn't sleep. It was a pretty dramatic turnaround from the teenaged girl who'd planned to put the license plate IMPLSIV on her car.

The anxiety grew unbearable, and I couldn't tamp it down, no matter how many controlling coping mechanisms I indulged in. The more I indulged in my compulsions, the worse they seemed to get. Driving home to check that garage door didn't scratch the itch in any permanent way; it just irritated the condition.

So I started drinking again—socially, I told myself, ignoring what I knew, which is that alcoholics and addicts can't drink socially. First it was a beer on the weekends. Then it was a beer when I got home from work. Then it was more beers, and some weed on the weekends. It wasn't long before I was back to my old ways, drinking and using drugs to find oblivion. I made the choice never to do meth again, but it sure wasn't clean and sober living.

I felt indescribable shame when I relapsed. My parents

had been so thrilled with my sobriety that they practically burst with pride whenever they saw me. It was many years before I could tell them.

I stopped going to AA and NA meetings. A meeting was exactly where I needed to be, of course, but I was too disgusted with myself to go. How could I tell everyone in my sober community that I'd started drinking and doing drugs again?

And the tentative relationship that I'd begun to build with God in rehab fell right to pieces. Instead of turning to Him and asking for help, I thought, *Who am I to have a relationship with God?* In my own eyes, I was a weak, lying piece of garbage. I'd disappointed everyone in my life, and the one good thing I'd ever done—getting clean—hadn't lasted. Why would He want anything to do with me? It was like dating in high school. I rejected Him before He could reject me.

Not surprisingly, Allen and I began to have problems. He was young and not sure he was ready yet for a long-term relationship. But the bigger issue was that he could see what I couldn't, which was that I hadn't done the work to get my life back. He loved me, but he could see it wouldn't be enough if I didn't love myself.

One night at the end of 2008, I got drunk, and Allen and I had a huge fight. We ended up in the parking lot of a Home Depot at two o'clock in the morning, screaming at each other. I got so mad, I hit him. Then I hit him again. I threw myself at him, clawing at his chest with my nails until his shirt was hanging in tatters right off him.

147

He didn't even push me back, which enraged me more, so I gathered myself and then slammed him as hard as I possibly could against the cement wall, knocking the wind right out of him and splitting open his head.

The sound of his head hitting the bricks and the sight of that streak of blood, so vivid against the orange wall, were unforgettable. Sickened by what I'd done, I realized that after years of being in abusive relationships, I'd become the abuser. Allen broke up with me that night, and he was right to do it. And then I was left alone with myself.

When I was crawling around on my knees in that roach-infested drug house before I went to rehab, I'd had the clarity to tell God that I knew I couldn't do my life by myself. "Please, God, help," I'd said. "I can't do it by myself, God. If I continue to control my own life, I'm going to die."

I meant it at the time, but I had no idea what it meant to let God have dominion in my life, to let Him into the dark corners.

I was white-knuckling it, thinking I could do it all myself. But of course I couldn't. None of us can. Because I was clean, I thought I was in charge. What resulted is what always happens when we think we're in charge of our own lives instead of handing the reins over to Him, namely chaos and destruction.

There wasn't any order, any depth, or true meaning to my days, because I had not let Him in. I wasn't praying in a real way or declaring my relationship with Him to myself and others. I wasn't dedicating my life to serving others in His name. And there's only so long you can tread water like that.

I didn't get clean after that night with Allen, but one particularly bad night months later served as a wake-up call for me. Afterward, I had a long talk with my best friend, Katie. She told me how scared she was for me and reminded me of how much I was loved. It's something she tells me often, to this day. But her words had a particular impact on me that day: I heard her.

It took a little while, but, once again (and for the last time, God willing), I got clean.

I've been asked a lot why I think I was able to get (and stay) clean that last time. For years, I didn't have a good answer. Then, in one of his sermons, my pastor differentiated between two kinds of sins: sinning out of weakness, and sinning out of willfulness.

That made sense to me. In the first years of my drug use after the rape, I was chasing Satan. I wanted annihilation, obliteration, destruction. I was searching out pain and violence, for myself and others.

It's true that when I fell back into drugs and alcohol after graduating from inpatient rehab, I did fall, and I did fail. But in those early, unsteady years, I was honestly trying to find a better way. When I started drinking and doing drugs again after rehab, I wasn't trying to punish myself or the world, or express rage at having my control taken away. I was just lost. I didn't know how to do better, but I wanted to. That, I think, is why God got underneath me and lifted me up.

As I'd already figured out, simply cleaning up didn't get rid of any of the underlying issues. My life still felt flat, without texture or meaning. I slept more and more, always a sign of depression for me. I'd be doing laundry or driving to work, and I'd think, *Is this all there is? There has to be more to it than this.*

God was listening then, too.

## CHAPTER TEN

# *Praise You in the Storm*

O ne day at the end of 2010, I was at my parents' house for dinner. I was helping my mom in the kitchen afterward, and she startled me with a question: Did I have any interest in going with her to a few churches in the area, to see if any of them were a good fit?

Unbeknownst to me, my mother had begun to renew her own faith. She'd always felt close to God, but she was beginning to realize that she wanted—needed—more. She had come to feel that she needed church in her life, a home base where she could delve deeper into her relationship with God and become part of a larger community of people doing the same.

I said yes—although I was less interested in finding a church than I was in taking some steps toward repairing my relationship with my mother.

Our relationship had been better since I'd gotten clean, but it wasn't entirely mended. After all that had happened between us, she still didn't fully trust me. I'd simply put her through too much. For my part, I had a tremendous amount of guilt over the lies I'd told her about going back to drugs and alcohol. (I still do.) Though she'd been so proud of me for getting clean, there was still a distance between us. We didn't laugh and hang out as easily as we had because she was always a little bit on guard with me, unwilling to let me all the way in. I thought that going to church with her would be a way to show my mom that I was truly back.

Unfortunately, the early churches my mother and I tried felt cliquish. We thought it might be easier to fit into a smaller congregation than at one of the huge megachurches, but neither one of us ever felt welcomed at the ones we tried. My mom was more motivated than I was, and therefore more likely to give a place a second or third chance, but I was disappointed by the whole experience. Impatient, I'd hoped and expected to feel more drastic changes sooner, and I used the lack of connection we were feeling at those smaller churches to stop going altogether. I did start praying a little on my own, though.

It was a hard time. My life felt so empty. I missed Allen terribly, though I knew we weren't right for each other. I also knew that I needed some time alone without a boyfriend; whatever was missing in my life, it wasn't a man. But the loneliness was crippling me.

One night that winter, I had a strange experience. It was a Friday night, and I was alone, taking a shower. Standing under the hot water, I started to cry, and then to pray. *I'm clean again, God, but something's still missing. I'm so, so lonely. Show me what it is that I need.*

I stayed there until the hot water ran out and I'd spent my tears. *Another fun Friday night at Alisa's house,* I thought as I climbed into my bathrobe. *Come for the snacks, stay for the breakdown with God in the shower.*

But as I started to towel off my hair, I had the feeling of a pair of hands resting on my shoulders. It wasn't a creepy feeling at all, but an intensely comforting one. It was a touch of love, and forgiveness, and comfort. The only description that sounds right is to say that it felt like home.

I knew immediately that I was in the presence of my grandfather. I had never truly processed his death. As I've said, he passed two weeks before that night at the beach house. (It was a blessing that my grandpa had died when he did. He would have killed the guys who assaulted me; it's better that he never knew.) That night, I felt him with me, his spirit filling a void in me and lifting the ache of loneliness that had been my near-constant companion for so long. I felt that God had sent him to comfort me.

It was such a tremendous gift to be able to have one more chance to tell my grandfather how much I loved and missed him. I told him how very sorry I was that I had not properly mourned his death. And that night, as I fell into a deep, refreshing sleep, that wonderful sense of companionship and forgiveness stayed with me.

That moment in my bathroom made me feel like I'd been given a view of a much better place. It was only a stone's throw away, but I had to get there, and I didn't know how.

\*    \*    \*

In April 2011, my mother signed us up for a women's retreat through my aunt Kathy's church. It was up in the mountains.

I was surprised she'd signed us up without talking to me first—and, frankly, more than a little bit annoyed. The retreat meant an entire weekend away, in the middle of nowhere. What would I do if I hated it?

My mom is smart. She didn't tell me that I had to go. She simply mentioned that she'd already sent a check to cover the two of us, and that she'd lose the deposit if I didn't show up. At that point, I was trying to show her I was committed to fixing our relationship, so I agreed to the trip.

But I wasn't happy about it, and when the Friday we were supposed to leave arrived, I was secretly relieved to hear that there was a massive snowstorm up in the mountains. We didn't have chains on our tires, and without them, there was no way to get up there.

"Too bad. I guess we can't go," I said. But my mom was dedicated; while she was waiting for me to get off work, she got snow chains put on her car. Then we discovered that the roads up the mountain were so dangerous, the highway patrol had shut them right down; you couldn't get through, even with the chains. We talked to my aunt, who was already up there, and she confirmed that the driving conditions were terrible.

"Next time," she said, eliciting another secret sigh of relief from me.

I tried to console my mother. "Bummer, Mom. But if the road is closed, there's nothing we can do. They'll give you your money back."

My mom wasn't giving up that easily. She says now that she had a feeling about it: "God wants Alisa there." So she woke up the next morning, Saturday, at first light, and called the highway patrol. Sure enough, there had been a thaw, and the roads up the mountain were open again. We were on our way.

I got in the car and sulked like a sullen teenager. I thought I'd been granted a reprieve. After I was done whining about how early it was, I fell asleep in the passenger seat, leaving my mom to do all the driving on the treacherously slippery roads. She'd chosen a less-steep back route, but we'd only made it a third of the way up before the highway patrol closed that road down, too.

Still, my mom did not head for home. Instead, she pulled over to the side of the road for a bit, and then she drove on back down the mountain and stopped at a Target for some shopping. Late afternoon, she got word that they'd opened the road again. Once again, we were on our way.

I had woken up by then and was in a completely horrendous mood. How much effort were we going to expend in getting up this mountain for this stupid retreat? It should have been a two-hour trip, and it had taken us the better part of two days. We finally arrived at the retreat center around dinner, by which time I had fully regressed to my horrible, teenaged self. I refused to get out of the car.

155

"Go in without me," I told my mom. "I want to sleep." I was in no mood to meet a bunch of random strangers, especially since they'd all been bonding together since the night before. "But you'll miss dinner!" my mom protested. "That's kind of the point," I said, shrugging the blanket up over me.

My mom let dinner slide, but she was not prepared to let me sleep through the two speakers scheduled for the after-dinner slot. I woke up to her shaking me, hard. "I'm not going to let you do this. You are not sleeping the whole weekend. I can see that you don't want to be here, but you are here, so get over it. You are going to participate."

I rolled my eyes but slouched in after her. My aunt was completely embarrassed. She'd been so excited that we'd agreed to come, and now I was shaming her in front of her church community by making it clear I was there against my will.

I slumped down in my seat, arms crossed over my chest, not caring what I looked like or what anyone thought. And I'm embarrassed to admit that I have absolutely no idea what the first speaker talked about. I couldn't hear her over the voice inside of me that was cursing my mom and my aunt and the stupid luck that had brought me to this stupid conference center on this stupid mountain with all these stupid people telling their stupid stories.

I marinated in that nasty mood for a good long while. But the second speaker's story caught my attention, and I found myself listening in spite of my foul temper.

Grace told us that her son had died at seventeen. He

was the light of her life, her reason for living. Her marriage wasn't great, but she'd stuck it out for the sake of her son. Her job wasn't great, but she kept it because she wanted to be able to provide for him. And he was a terrific kid: sweet, popular, good-looking, a straight-A student, and an athlete—until just before Christmas, on his way to pick up presents for the family, when a speeding car cut him off on the freeway, forcing his car off the road. He died at the scene.

Grace told us that, after his death, she went completely off the rails. She told us how angry she'd been at God for taking her beloved son. She told us how much she hated his best friend for surviving the accident, and all the ways that she fantasized about trading the friend's death for her own son's life. It was dark, deep, painful stuff.

When she was starting to crawl out of her grief and find a place of healing, her daughter, who was of course also struggling with the death of her brother, started getting into drugs and alcohol. The daughter's problem became a serious one. After trying everything, Grace realized—as my mother had—that there was nothing she could do to help her except cut her off. When Grace described that time in her life, she made a very simple statement that I'll never forget as long as I live. She said, "I'd had two children, and both of them were lost."

Hearing her say that, I understood what my parents had gone through while I was using drugs. My biggest revelation of that weekend didn't have anything to do with me or with the rape. It was the thought of my parents and what I'd put them through—not only with the trials, but the aftermath with my drug use and erratic behavior bordering on suicide. I was overwhelmed with terrible guilt and retroactive terror.

Then, as if someone had switched on a light, I could see clearly that I could be forgiven for everything I'd done to my parents and to myself and to everyone else, if only I could ask for forgiveness. For the first time, I understood that Jesus had died so that I might have a new start. All I had to do was trust Him and give myself over to Him.

I can't describe it except to say that I felt different—lighter, somehow—as if someone had presented me with the perfect solution to a problem I'd been struggling fruitlessly with for years. People were milling around about me, hugging each other in fellowship and going up to hug Grace, but I sat very still in my chair, as if moving too fast would startle the understanding right out of me.

The leaders of the retreat led us in prayer. To close, they played us a song, "Praise You in the Storm," by the Christian band Casting Crowns. In it, the singer expresses his dismay that the terrible storm outside is still raging. He confesses that he doesn't think he can go on, but he does not lose hope. Although he feels abandoned, he knows that he is not alone. I listened carefully. The lyrics were beautiful to me, a perfect expression of what it feels like to be struggling and afraid, sure that God has forsaken you.

For years, I had been searching and searching for something—anything—to take the pain away. I had lost years to drugs and abusive relationships and to a mechanical, dry sobriety, with very little joy or meaning in it. Between

Grace's speech and this song, I was being led, very gently, toward the path that would deliver me out of all the pain I was in. The answer was right there in front of me. All I had to do was praise Him.

I went to bed quickly, without saying anything to my mom or to my aunt. I'd been so difficult all day, they were giving me a fairly wide berth anyway. I needed a little space to fully understand what I'd just been given a quick glimpse of. Had I truly heard what I'd heard? And if it was that simple, could I do it? Could I turn my life over to God?

I hardly slept, tossing and turning with questions. The next morning, I came into the main room of the retreat to find a number of craft tables set up. I like to do crafts. I'm not super-talented artistically, but I am visual, and I find it very meditative to create with my hands—especially when I have a lot on my mind, as I did that morning.

I sat down at one of the tables, where a woman was showing a group how to make a simple angel shape out of pipe cleaners and beads. I chose pipe cleaners and beads in all my favorite colors for my angel—shell pink, purple, hot pink, baby blue, and black—and I gave her a glittery silver crown. When I was done, I sat back and looked at the little angel I'd made and felt very pleased with my handiwork. I had no idea how significant she would become—the first in what would become a collection of angels, and a constant reminder of the most important weekend in my life.

During the session at the very end of the retreat, the

leader asked if there was anybody who wanted to accept Jesus Christ as their Lord and Savior. Almost everybody else there had accepted Him already, and I'd been such a whiny pain the whole weekend that nobody even looked over at me. My mom and aunt were barely speaking to me by that point.

I knew I wanted to stand up, but I was scared. All of a sudden, I found myself on my feet. I heard my mom gasp and start to cry, and my aunt followed suit. My heart beat in my chest so hard I thought for sure everyone could hear it.

That Sunday, April 10, 2011, I stood up and turned my life over to God. I pledged to trust Him, and I asked for that forgiveness.

Standing up there was one of the most frightening moments of my life. The guilt I felt for so many years had given me some measure of control, and some days that fantasy of control was the only thing keeping me sane. Asking for forgiveness and letting Him into my life meant giving up that control. But I could see that it also meant freedom, relief from the loneliness and pain and guilt that I'd carried around with me for so long. When I said that yes, I would take Jesus Christ as my Lord and Savior, the feeling I had can only be described as pure, unadulterated joy.

There were lots of hugs all around, and then my aunt gestured for me to wait while she ran back to her room. She came back carrying a pink Bible. She'd bought it for me before the weekend, but I'd behaved so abominably that she'd planned to take it home with her again. She'd marked a passage for me. In the passage, God speaks to Jeremiah:

"For I know the plans I have for you," declares the LORD, "plans to prosper you and not to harm you, plans to give you hope and a future. Then you will call on me and come and pray to me, and I will listen to you. You will seek me and find me when you seek me with all your heart. I will be found by you," declares the LORD, "and will bring you back from captivity. I will gather you from all the nations and places where I have banished you," declares the LORD, "and will bring you back to the place from which I carried you into exile." (Jeremiah 29:11–15, NIV)

It was another step down the path to righteousness. The word *exile* seemed so right to me—the perfect way to describe the way I'd felt since the rape. But here it was, a promise in His own words: No matter how deep the exile or how profound the loneliness, God would bring me back.

My conversion story was not dramatic. One afternoon, I was sitting in traffic on the 405, listening to the radio and thinking about what I was going to have for dinner, and I understood that God was with me. After that day, I never lost Him again.

## CHAPTER ELEVEN

# *I Will Bring You Back*

After that retreat in the mountains, my life changed. Accepting God into my life gave my whole life a deepness and richness that had been missing. The shoot that had always been curled inside of me finally had the space and light it needed to grow. And once I wasn't neglecting this side of myself, I found that it flourished.

God had delivered me back to myself, the person I was meant to be. Not the person I was meant to be before the rape—that girl was gone—but the woman who had survived it.

I'd already learned the hard way that I couldn't skate along in my sobriety. I had to show up to do what Tina had called the footwork.

It wasn't easy. I had to feel, really *feel*, the grief and violation that I'd been numb to after the rape and throughout the two trials, and I had to manage those feelings. I had to grieve for the perfectionist who thought she'd change New York and the world with her hard-hitting, ground-breaking journalism. And I had to do that at the same time that I was trying to forgive the broken drug addict who thought nothing of smoking meth in the same room as a baby's crib.

It was—to put it mildly—a lot to handle. But I had help.

First, I'd found a great therapist. She specialized in post-traumatic stress disorder. Many war veterans exhibit symptoms of PTSD, but it is also common in people who have experienced many different kinds of trauma. Basically, people who suffer from PTSD respond—emotionally, psy-chologically, and often physically—as if they are in danger, long after the danger has passed. It was a huge relief to dis-cover that my thoughts and feelings, as well as many of my controlling behaviors, were common and treatable; I had thought I was the only one. Plus, knowing that I could go to my therapist's office to talk about everything that still hurt was very freeing for me, and it gave me the freedom to start to think about a more outward-facing life.

Then, in May 2011, my mom and I found a church we loved.

It's called Water of Life. It has about fourteen thousand members and three campuses. The main worship center seats more than a thousand people, and there are three video centers available at the main campus, as well as a Spanish-language service. Between four thousand and five thousand people attend the various services every Sunday.

163

Finding Water of Life happened in a funny way. My aunt knew we were having some difficulty finding a home church in our area, and she encouraged us to try Water of Life. She'd heard good things from churchgoers she trusted, and thought it would be a good match for us because of the emphasis on Bible study. I'd been raised without any religion at all and hadn't learned even the most basic Bible stories, even the ones most six-year-olds in Sunday school know. I had quite a lot to catch up on. But my mom and I didn't think we'd be happy at Water of Life because the congregation was so big. We were worried that it would feel too impersonal.

My aunt kept bringing it up, and I finally checked out the website. Needless to say, I was pretty amazed by what I saw there. This church had Bible study groups for everything you could think of. There were groups for those grieving a loss, for people going through a divorce, for single moms, for addicts in recovery.

Then I saw a listing that took my breath away: Water of Life offered a special Bible study group—a free, three-month-long session—designed specifically for survivors of sexual assault.

Now, I'd pretty much given up on finding a support group for sexual assault survivors in my area. Even Project Sister, the rape crisis center where I would come to volunteer, didn't host any. The scarcity of support groups for rape survivors is both a symptom of and a contributor to the shame rape victims feel about coming forward. So many people can't talk about what happened to them. And then when they're ready, it's hard to find a safe place to do it. So when I saw that Water of Life had a Bible Study group specifically for sexual assault survivors, I took it as a sign.

I didn't sign up for the group right away, but my mom and I knew we'd found our spiritual home on the very first Sunday we attended church. It felt so hospitable and open, in surprising contrast to some of the smaller churches we tried. It seemed congregants would go out of their way to greet us, precisely because we were faces they didn't recognize. And there were so many things to do. The course catalog read like a Christmas list; I couldn't decide which programs I wanted to join first. They even offered Zumba on Monday nights.

But the biggest factor in our decision to join Water of Life was Pastor Dan.

Pastor Dan is open about his troubled past; in his sermons, he talks about breaking into houses as a kid, about his drug use and being sent to military school. (A weird part of the story: My mom and aunt knew him in high school. When my mom told my aunt that he was the pastor at Water of Life, my aunt said, shocked, "Danny the druggie?")

His candor surprised me in those early weeks and helped me feel that I belonged at Water of Life. This pastor wasn't someone handing down wisdom from up high, but someone who had fought his way out of the devil's grip. This wasn't someone who'd always led a cushy, God-filled life, but someone who most likely knew what it was like to wake up in a seedy motel, wondering where the day's drugs would come from. I know there isn't a church in the world led by someone who hasn't sinned, but when Pastor Dan says that God loves us, no matter what we have done or how we feel about ourselves, I can really hear it as true.

Pastor Dan also spoke very freely and honestly about a topic I'd been struggling with since I got clean, which is that staying in your faith can be hard. At all the other churches we'd gone to, it seemed the faithful were having a much easier time than I was. They didn't seem to struggle with God, to question Him or the path He'd chosen for them. It certainly didn't seem like any of the people at those other churches had ever yelled at Him, as I was sometimes tempted to do. This had made me feel rotten, like I was a bad Christian, like I was doing it wrong. I was trying my hardest. Why wasn't it easier for me?

Pastor Dan's sermons dealt with these issues head-on. He talked about the struggle, the fight to stay committed to one's faith. He talked about temptation and about failure. He talked about Jacob, who stayed up all night wrestling with God. He talked about Jeremiah, about Job, about Paul. Listening, I began to understand that my pain and turmoil were part of walking with Him. As long as I did not turn away but kept seeking Him, I would be all right.

Going to church gave me the spiritual practice I'd been missing, everyday guidance on how to be restored to a right relationship with God and how to live my daily life walking with Him. I wanted to build a relationship with God, and Sunday mornings felt like quality time with

Him. Church gave me a space to express the gratitude I felt and the struggles I still held in my heart, and served as a much-needed reflection.

The sermon for the week invariably blew me away. I'd never studied the Bible in such depth before—in fact, I'd never studied anything in such depth before. I often felt that I'd learned more during the sermon than I had all week at college. And what I learned Sunday morning gave me a context for everything I was doing, whether at work, in my relationships, or in my sobriety.

I learned quickly how much better I felt if I woke up every morning a little early to read the Bible before work. The depth and richness of scripture astonished me. No matter what was on my mind, it seemed that I could find a story or a quote that spoke directly to me. I wore out a lot of highlighters. I felt comforted to discover that everything I needed had always been there.

That said, reading the Bible can be difficult, especially if you didn't grow up doing it. I had to remind myself to be patient; after all, I was encountering a lot of the stories and ideas for the first time. When I'd first picked up the Bible, in rehab, it was overwhelming to hit dense passages, stories I didn't immediately understand. But being part of a church community, especially one that puts a lot of emphasis on Bible study, helped me to keep going. It certainly taught me that I can always ask for help. It also taught me that I may have a completely different understanding of a story from one year to the next. I realized that I have a whole lifetime ahead of me to learn what I don't yet know.

After we joined Water of Life, the terrible loneliness I'd been feeling abated. Partly I think that was because I started to join groups at the church and make friends. Being with other like-minded people of faith felt like a balm to my soul after so much solitude. Losing my high school friends was one of the most painful things that happened in the aftermath of my rape, and it was the one that left the deepest scar. I came to see that I hadn't had a deep friendship since.

For years, the closest people to me had been a succession of abusive boyfriends and drug buddies. My boyfriends and drug buddies were good at showing up when they needed drugs or money or a place to crash, and sometimes they were even good at showing up for me when I needed those things. Drug addicts are always in survival mode (survival meant drugs) and that often meant that we didn't have a whole lot left over for friendship. I certainly wasn't a very good friend when I was using. But I had been lonely—deeply, painfully lonely—much of the time.

The relief I felt when the loneliness lifted was a drink of icy cold water on the hottest day of the year. Ironically, it also meant that, for the first time in my life, I didn't mind being by myself. I'd always needed to have a crowd around—noise, action, distractions—because I didn't feel comfortable in my own skin. Suddenly I found that I was perfectly happy to sit quietly with the Bible or a book of daily devotions. I knew that God was right there with me, and His presence allowed me to find some peace. It also allowed me to make some real friendships—and to renew some old ones.

One afternoon, my phone rang.

"Alisa?"

My phone said it was my mom's cell phone calling. But the voice at the other end wasn't my mom's. It did seem familiar, though.

"It's me, Alisa. It's Beka."

You could have heard my scream of joy and delight in Oregon.

I'd tried to find Beka when I got clean, but she'd moved and her number had changed. Then, providentially, my parents had run into her at the hospital where she works as a nurse. She was at work, so we agreed to talk later. And when we did, it was like we were picking up right where we'd left off, ten years before.

Beka hadn't changed. She still knew all the gossip about everyone; she was still the person who'd throw you a baby shower or organize everyone to come together for your birthday. She was exactly the same—except in one important way.

"You'll never believe it," she said. "But I've started going to church."

"Me too!" I exclaimed.

It took about thirty seconds for us to figure out that, although we'd never seen each other there, we were both attending Water of Life. So Beka and I became church buddies. Since my mom and I had joined, I had wanted to go to a program called Pure, a ministry for younger people between eighteen and twenty-nine, but I'd never had the nerve to go by myself. I started going with Beka. And we started going to Zumba class on Monday nights, too.

God had delivered me back to myself. I was finally—finally!—doing the footwork, and it was as if everything that had been random and chaotic in my life began to fall into place. A whole world was opening up to me, and I felt the comfort that comes from learning that I could, at long last, put down the heavy burdens I had carried for so long.

The little angel I made at that first retreat in the mountains hangs from a lamp in my bedroom.

She's since been joined by many other little angels, mostly gifts from people who love me, and each one of them is significant in its own way. My little pipe-cleaner angel may not be as lovely as some of the others, but there's a reason she's one of the first things I see when I walk into my bedroom.

That little angel reminds me that I am the child of a good and all-powerful God, and that I was created in His image. Most importantly, she reminds me that He has a purpose—a perfect plan—for me on this earth.

The respite I found at church allowed me to begin to explore my calling, the plan God had for me.

Even after I had found my faith and my place in a church community, I found that I still struggled mightily with the many ways that the rape had disrupted my life. Even after so many years had passed, I kept wondering: *Why me, Lord, why me?* It felt like I was bashing my head against a wall. I knew He loved me. So how could I reconcile that with what had happened to me?

A passage from Isaiah that I read one morning helped me along the way toward understanding:

People of Zion, who live in Jerusalem, you will weep no more. How gracious he will be when you cry for help! As soon as he hears, he will answer you. Although the Lord gives you the bread of adversity and the water of affliction, your teachers will be hidden no more; with your own eyes you will see them. Whether you turn to the right or to the left, your ears will hear a voice behind you, saying, "This is the way; walk in it." (Isaiah 30:19–21 NIV)

That concept was an eye-opener for me. It was only through my suffering that I had truly come to know God. Had He used adversity to bring me closer to Him? Maybe He hadn't been punishing me with everything that happened, but simply trying to get me to know Him. Maybe He had work He needed me to do.

For years, I had been so wrapped up in my own pain and struggles that I hadn't been in touch with a fundamentally important part of me: the part that wants—and needs—to help other people. That was what I had loved about being a Girl Scout and why I'd stayed with the Scouts for years. It was why I'd taken such pride in being a good friend as I grew up. But it was also a part of myself that I had completely lost touch with as I sank into depression and drug addiction after my rape.

As my healing progressed, that started to change.

Going to church put the concept of service back where it belonged, right in front of me. Service is huge at Water of Life. There's an understanding that the most important thing you can do is serve God and help others in whatever way that you can. Pastor Dan is fond of saying, "He doesn't touch us so that we can be touched, but so that we can touch others." At Water of Life, you can help by going on a mission to an underdeveloped country, by sending money to sponsor children who otherwise might not have access to the nutrition and education they need, or simply by helping to direct traffic in the church parking lot on a busy Sunday morning.

For me, the drive to serve came from a simple place. I was conscious every day that I'd been given this huge gift— my life!—and I knew I couldn't squander it; I needed to do something with it. I needed to show my gratitude to God, and to everyone who had helped me, by making my life the most joyful and meaningful one I could.

I think there was a selfish aspect to this as well. Being of service is a profound way for trauma survivors to heal. Whenever someone asked the children's television personality Mr. Rogers how to talk to their kids about scary events happening in the world and on the news, he would say that his own mother used to tell him, "Look for the helpers. There are always people helping."

I think about that a lot. In my experience, it's true: There are always people helping. After 9/11, firefighters from all around the country traveled to New York to help in any way they could. So many people lined up to donate blood that the Red Cross had to turn them away. Just the other day, when I was at the mall, I saw an elderly woman lose her footing and fall. In a matter of seconds, there were so many people surrounding her—trying to help her up, offering to reach out to her family or call for help—that it quickly became clear that the rest of us weren't needed at all.

The helpers had been there for me, too. My parents, my lawyers, Shirley and Tiare, Susan, Tina, the other aides at all the rehabs I'd gone to—they were there, and ready to do anything they could to help me. For a long time, I couldn't accept the help they were offering. But when I'd been able to reach out and grab hold of the life preserver they'd thrown out to me, those people had pulled me in.

With solid ground under my feet, I felt I might be ready to try to pull someone else to safety. It was very empowering to realize that I was the person who could help—as opposed to the one who needed it.

I was ready to feel good again. It's a dirty little secret, but being of service feels fantastic. It lines you up with what you believe in, the values and beliefs that light you up. I believe with every fiber of my being that God gave me my specific talents and experiences—all of them—so that I could use them to serve other people. Now that I was back on my feet, I needed to figure out how best to do that.

I started pretty small. If a co-worker needed me to stay late to finish a project, or my parents needed me to do them a favor, I showed up for them. My act of service might be as simple as braking so that someone could pull into heavy traffic in front of me. No matter how insignificant the act seemed, I was always grateful for the opportunity, and I dedicated it to God.

I had also adopted a dog, an Australian and German shepherd mix, a shelter rescue named Daisy. I fell head over heels in love with her, and she quickly became the center of my life.

Daisy had been badly abused and fed more junk food than dog food, which had left her so uncomfortably over-weight that she could barely move. I took a tremendous amount of pride in restoring her to a normal weight, not to mention to full health and confidence. When I woke up in the morning, I fed Daisy before I fed myself. When I got home at night from work and school, we went out for a good long walk—and she got to sniff every tree, even if I was so exhausted I could barely stay upright.

One short year before, I'd been in no position to rescue anyone. But after I'd taken Jesus into my heart, it felt right to put someone else's needs—even a dog's—before my own.

Helping felt great and somehow natural to me, and

helped to build my confidence. These particular acts of service may not have been super-significant in the grand scheme of things, but I used them to get back in shape, to build my good works muscles. I knew that I would feel another degree better once I landed on a way to serve that I could dedicate my life to.

I was still struggling over what I was going to do with my life, professionally. I'd gone back to college a couple of years before. That had been a huge step in the right direction, of course, but I hadn't been able to make it work for me. I'd been drifting around, taking classes in various areas, but none of them had meant anything to me on a fundamental level, and so nothing had stuck.

I started to pray on it. God had saved my life; what did He want me to do with it? I knew that I wanted to help people. How could I best do that?

I prayed a lot. Then, one morning, reading my Bible, I found myself returning over and over to this line from Corinthians:

Praise be to the God and Father of our Lord Jesus Christ, the Father of compassion and the God of all comfort, who comforts us in all our troubles, so that we can comfort those in any trouble with the comfort we ourselves receive from God. (2 Corinthians 1:3–4, NIV)

I couldn't get it out of my head: "so that we can comfort those in any trouble with the comfort we ourselves receive."

I suddenly found that I knew exactly what God wanted me to do: He wanted me to comfort others, as He had comforted me. Who better to help women who had been raped or abused than someone who knew exactly what they'd been through?

I picked up my phone and called my own personal angel and victim's advocate, Tiare. She agreed to meet me at her office to talk about some career options, and I walked out of there knowing I wanted to try to become a victim's advocate.

That decision galvanized everything in my life. I spent hours paging through the course catalog at the community college I was attending, and I signed up for my next semester's courses with renewed purpose, taking classes in criminal justice and the psychology of violence. I didn't have to pinch myself to stay awake in these classes or bribe myself to do the reading. Unlike the history of film, or some random sociology class, these were subjects I already felt intensely and passionately about.

Tiare also suggested that I begin volunteering at a center that helps victims of sexual assault. She even picked the one I ended up volunteering for, Project Sister Family Services, in Los Angeles County. *SISTER* stands for Sisters in Service to End Rape, which the organization has been working to do since it was founded in the early seventies. The services Project Sister provides include a twenty-four-hour hotline and victim advocacy work, including accompanying victims to their medical exams, interviews with police, and court appearances. There's an education piece, too, to go along with the advocacy. People from the organization give presentations in schools about sexual assault, offer self-defense classes and an antiviolence program for pregnant and parenting teens, and do outreach with high-risk youth. It was a place I wanted to be a part of.

That was an intense period in my life. I was working full time. Two nights a week, I went to classes, and another two nights a week, I did the training for Project Sister. I need eight hours of sleep a night, and I wasn't getting anywhere near that amount, but I powered through. I knew I was taking important steps toward what I wanted to do, and I wanted all of it so badly that I found I could stay positive and focused on my goals, even on the hard days. I wasn't drifting anymore.

Everyone in my life was thrilled to see that I was getting my life back on track. A couple of weeks after I decided to become a victim's advocate, I got a call from Shirley, asking if we could meet for lunch. Since I'd gotten clean, we'd become very close; she and my mom and I would often meet up to go shopping together or for a meal. It meant a lot to me that she'd been supportive when she'd heard about my experience at the retreat in the mountains and the news that I was regularly attending church. As a person of faith herself, she knew it was the right thing, and she took an almost maternal pride in the transformation that was taking place in me. And of course, she'd been over the moon with excitement when she heard that I was planning to follow in her footsteps professionally.

At lunch, Shirley dropped a bombshell. After forty years

of helping victims, she was retiring to spend more time with her grandkids, and she had something she wanted to give me.

The box she pushed across the table toward me was gorgeous: thick, textured pink paper, with a beautiful white cut-paper flower on the top. The box was so pretty, I thought it was the present.

"Open it," she said.

Inside, there was a smooth, clear crystal, oval like a river stone, and the perfect size to fit into a small person's palm.

I knew what it was. Shirley had given this clear stone to every one of her victims to hold while they were on the stand. It was deliberately small enough to be carried, unnoticed, in the palm of a victim's hand. Shirley would push the stone into your palm, saying: "This is the hardest thing you'll ever do, and you are so strong for doing it. Hold this crystal while you're up there, and put all of your strength into it, and I'll pass it along to the next girl who needs that strength. You'll be her strength, until she finds her own."

It was the crystal that had been taken away from me at my own trial.

The crystal was a reminder to victims that they were strong, at the very moment when they felt weakest. It was a call to service: If they couldn't be brave for themselves, they could be brave for other victims. It was a physical reminder that someone believed them and believed in them. And it was proof positive that there was an "after." Other victims had gone through the valley of the shadow of darkness, and they had gone on. They had given the crystal back to Shirley, and with it, a piece of their strength.

We hugged each other and cried. It was one of the most meaningful gifts I had ever received and became one of my most treasured possessions. I keep it on my dressing table, right in plain sight, so that I can never lose sight of what it means. I hold it myself sometimes, when I'm struggling and praying on the struggle.

In March 2012, I became a state-certified victim's advocate and crisis intervention counselor.

I volunteer about eighteen hours a month at Project Sister. I respond to crisis calls from women (and they are mostly women) who have been sexually assaulted. I spend a lot of time with their families, as long as their family members aren't the perpetrators of the crimes, counseling them on how they can help the survivor and what to do with their own feelings.

With the survivors, I mostly listen. I hug them if they want a hug and hold their hands if they want that contact. I stay with them during their medical exams, explaining every step, as Tiare did during my own. I tell them that I'll listen if they want to talk, and that I'll answer every question they have, if they have any. But mostly I tell them that I'm here to be here. I'm here so that you have somebody here who is just for you. I'm here to support you and to remind you that you're not alone. We will get through this, I tell them, and we will get through it together.

179

The question they always ask is, "Why did this happen to me? Why did he think it was okay to do this to me?" I don't have a good answer for that one, but I try to give them as much hope for the future as I possibly can. I understand what they are feeling because I have felt it, and often I can help them because I've been there myself. Better than anyone else, I know that sometimes all you can do is hold someone's hand while she cries.

Once I have my college degree, I will pursue a job as a victim's advocate in the district attorney's office. When I do, I'll take Shirley's crystal with me.

CHAPTER TWELVE

# *Transforming the Road*

I 'm often asked if it isn't difficult, given my history, to work with women who have been sexually assaulted and abused. Doesn't it bring up bad feelings and make it harder for me to move on?

The answer is no. I have been doing this work as a volunteer for a couple of years now, and I truly see it as my purpose in life. There is a passage in the book of James that I have marked so I can return to it whenever I need a reminder of why service is so important:

What good is it, my brothers and sisters, if someone claims to have faith but has no deeds? Can such faith save them? Suppose a brother or a sister is without clothes and daily food. If one of you says to them, "Go in peace; keep warm and well fed," but does nothing about their physical needs, what good is it? In the same way, faith by itself, if it is not accompanied by action, is dead. ( James 2:14–17, NIV)

That passage resonates strongly with me, probably because it echoes what my counselor Tina had always said about showing up and doing the footwork. You can get sober, but if you don't do the footwork, your sobriety is dead, even if you never touch another drop of alcohol or do another drug again.

The same thing is true about faith. It's my role, as a Christian, to bring light to the darkness. I honestly believe that if I'm not doing anything to serve God and my fellow humans, then I'm not doing everything I was put on this earth to do.

My work at Project Sister is hard, and it was even harder when I first started doing it. Some nights I'd go home from a shift and I'd cry until I didn't have any tears left. It still boggles my mind, the things that men do to women and girls, the things that human beings do to one another. Some of those nights, I didn't even want to belong to this species anymore. Dealing with the little kids is the hardest for me; I think that's true for most of us, including the advocates with twenty years of experience. Still, every time I pulled an all-nighter on the hotline or went to the hospital with a survivor, I knew I was doing something important, something that I was supposed to do.

I stayed mindful of the idea, though, that God gives us our specific talents and experiences so that we can use them to serve. I knew I was a good listener and that the women and girls I worked with felt heard and comforted by me. When I was younger, I'd always been the person my friends came to for sympathy and comfort, to cry with and to ask advice. I am good at keeping secrets, as long as they're the kind of secrets that should be kept, and I can listen with compassion and without judgment.

But as I got more experienced, I realized that I was as engaged with the educational work I was doing at Project Sister as I was with the accompaniment work. For instance, I felt called to spend time with the partners and family members of the survivors. We call the partners, friends, and parents of sexual assault victims "secondary survivors."

There was a lot to help with. Secondary survivors often feel surprised by the intensity of their own feelings. Secondary survivors have to deal with the fact that they weren't able to keep their loved ones safe. Isn't it the first thing we pray, that those we love stay out of harm's way? It's common for secondary survivors to feel deeply helpless and angry that they weren't able to offer protection, and they often benefit from finding someone of their own to talk to about those feelings.

As I knew too well from my own experience, secondary survivors often aren't sure what to say to the family member who has been hurt. But what families and friends do say is important. The support and love that a survivor receives, especially in the immediate aftermath of an assault, can be a huge factor in their recovery.

Families also need to understand that survivors may have difficulty, going forward, with intimacy and connection. I had a lot of problems with my dad in the immediate aftermath of my own rape—not because of anything in particular that he was doing, but simply because he was male.

I know that it helps when I can tell a victim's dad that he shouldn't take his daughter's anger or skittishness personally.

Working with the families helped me to see that while I wanted to keep helping victims on a case-by-case basis, I also wanted a broader reach. My case had been so extreme and so high profile, the media attention so ferocious. Why had I been given such a platform if I wasn't meant to try to bring these messages to as much of the world as possible?

That became my new quest, to answer this question: How could I tackle big issues—topics such as victim blaming, or a culture in which it's normal and accepted to reduce women to sexual objects—in a way that would not only benefit the specific girl whose hand I was holding, but a wider audience, too?

I kept volunteering, and I kept praying. I knew God would give me a chance.

A beautiful short video came out while the Steubenville rape case was still very much in the news. You can find it on YouTube.

"Hey, bros, check who passed out on the couch," a guy says to the camera. You can see an unconscious girl laid out on the sofa behind him. "Guess what I'm going to do to her," he says—and like most women watching, I felt my heart seize up. But then he turns around, puts a pillow under her head, covers her body with a blanket, and leaves a glass of water near the couch, where she can reach it.

He turns back to the camera and says, "Real men treat women with respect."

It's only twenty-six seconds long, but it's very powerful. One of the reasons it's so powerful is that it dares to ask why we settle for so little when we could ask for so much.

The story of the Good Samaritan is one of my absolute favorites in the Bible. I find it incredibly moving, a real testament to the power of humanity. I discovered recently that it was also one of Martin Luther King Jr.'s favorite stories in the Bible; he even references it in the famous "I Have a Dream" speech.

I found that, in some of his other writings, King goes a step further. Yes, of course we need more Good Samaritans, more people who are courageous enough to do the right thing when they come upon a person in need. But King suggests that the real work is in transforming the dangerous road to Jericho. Why should we have to live with the expectation of being beaten and robbed simply because we are traveling from one place to another?

I find this interpretation of the story inspiring. Like the Good Samaritan, every one of us needs to stop and help whenever the opportunity presents itself. But I also believe that we have to transform the road to Jericho by effecting bigger changes in the world. That is why that Steubenville video is so powerful. When a young man puts a blanket over a passed-out girl at a party, he's a Good Samaritan. But when he appears in a YouTube video that goes viral about respecting women, he's transforming the road to Jericho.

People like me, who talk to young women about how

to keep themselves safe, tend to put the onus of responsibility on the girl: We talk about how not to get raped. Don't wear provocative clothing, we say. Don't be promiscuous. Don't go into dangerous neighborhoods. Learn self-defense. Don't get so drunk or drugged that you can't function. Go in pairs. Take care of one another.

I'm not going to stop saying those things, because my goal is to keep as many young women as safe as I possibly can. Rape, Abuse and Incest National Network (RAINN) calls this risk reduction, and I believe in it. But when I speak at schools, I make sure to speak to the young men, too. Because the real way to end sexual assault is not to encourage women to dress less provocatively, but to get men to stop raping them.

To be clear, I don't think that men are, by definition, the problem. In fact, when we say "boys will be boys" and in all the other ways we apologize for unacceptable male behavior, we disrespect all the amazing men out there who know that it's not normal to rape someone just because they can. I'm proud to say that there are men in my life now who would be sickened by the very thought of taking advantage of someone who couldn't consent, and who wouldn't think twice before tucking a blanket over that passed-out girl. Indeed, men can be—and have to be—very powerful allies in our transformation of the road to Jericho. But we need to educate a lot more men and think long and hard about how we raise boys before it's a circumstance we can count on.

I still accompany sexual assault survivors to court and

to their medical exams; I still visit with their families. But I've also gotten more involved in the education outreach we do at Project Sister. In 2013, Project Sister announced they were adding a new volunteer advocate outreach and prevention group called Speakers to Educate and Prevent (STEP). Sophia, the outreach coordinator, asked if I would help lead the volunteers. My responsibilities would include giving presentations, training volunteers, and helping to develop ideas for presentations we'd be giving in the future.

It was a huge amount of work, but I jumped at the offer. The topics we cover include sexual assault, child abuse, healthy relationships, bullying, Internet safety, self-defense, mandated reporting, and good touch/bad touch. Once trained, the STEP volunteers take different presentations and materials to elementary schools, intermediate schools, high schools, and colleges. We go to city events and meetings, and to health fairs. We do corporate trainings and we go to law enforcement agencies, too.

The program has been an incredible success, and it's one of the most gratifying things that I do. I can see that we are changing people's minds and beliefs every time we speak. After we present the material, we open the floor up for a question-and-answer period, which is usually my favorite part. It's hard to realize how little the public knows about what it means to be a survivor of sexual assault. But I never mind any of the questions as long as we're engaged in a dialogue. For me, that's the most important thing.

And my work with STEP means I think a lot about how to talk to men, especially young men, about rape.

The first thing I do when I speak is to remind them that rape is *any* sexual contact without consent. (Shockingly, a lot of boys don't know this.) Oral sex without consent is rape. Touching someone without consent is rape. Using an object to touch someone without consent is rape. Having sex with someone who is under the age of consent is rape. I ask them: Do you know what the age of consent is? I'm always surprised by how few do.

And consent, I remind the young men I talk to, should be crystal clear. Just because she can't or hasn't said no doesn't mean you can assume consent. If she's drunk, assume it's a no. If she's giving in because you've been so persistent or because she needs a ride home, it's a no, too. Wouldn't you rather wait until it's an enthusiastic, no-question-about-it *yes*? We call this enthusiastic consent, and I think more young men—and young women—should know about it.

I also ask young men to think about their participation in the culture at large. We live in a world where, until a couple of months ago, on social media you could find a photo of a woman with her mouth taped shut and the words "Don't wrap it and tap it; tape her and rape her" superimposed on the image. I practically fell off my chair when I saw some of these: "Win her over with Chloroform." "What do you do after raping a deaf mute? Break her fingers so she can't tell anyone." You could buy a "Keep Calm and Rape" T-shirt from Amazon.com until shoppers protested. These are signs to me that the road to Jericho needs a little work.

So when I talk to young men, I ask them: Do you make rape jokes, or do you laugh when someone else does? Do you harass women on the street by yelling at them or making comments about the way they look? When you don't like a woman's opinion, is your default response to criticize the way she looks or dresses or to threaten her with sexual violence?

This is especially prevalent on the Internet, where the comment sections of websites are often filled with truly appalling, often violent invective against the woman featured in the article—simply because the commenter doesn't agree with her position on immigration reform or animal rights. Go spend ten minutes reading the comments on YouTube. (Actually, I take that back—I wouldn't wish YouTube comments on my worst enemy. Take my word for it, and go look at pictures of puppies instead.)

I also remind the guys I speak to not to trivialize the experience of rape when they hear about it. Unfortunately, statistically speaking, most of them will know a sexual assault victim in their lives. Don't blame the victim by asking questions like "What was she wearing?" or "What was she doing at that party by herself anyway?"

I remind them to be Good Samaritans if they can and not to be bystanders. "If something is happening that shouldn't be, stand up and do something, and if you hear about an assault, contact the authorities."

Most importantly, I tell them, never forget that the women in your life are people.

If we are serious about change, these are the conversations

that all of us have to have with our sons and nephews—with all the young men in our lives. We have to talk about these issues.

A woman came up to me once after I had spoken at a health fair. "You better believe our whole family is sitting down tonight to talk about what I've heard here today," she told me. "Not just the girl, but the boy, too." I felt so good about inspiring her to have that conversation with her kids—one that might just lead to a slightly better, safer world.

Are these easy talks to have? They certainly aren't. Most of us would rather sweep these issues under the rug and pretend that rape happens to other people in other places. But education and prevention do work. We need to stand together now and shine a light. Together, I believe that we can transform the road.

# CHAPTER THIRTEEN

## *Speaking Out*

I n 2011, God gave me a great way to do my part in transforming the road. It would take another year before I could find the courage to take Him up on it, though.

Right after the retreat with my aunt Kathy's church in the mountains, Susan Schroeder, chief of staff at the DA's office, called me. We'd stayed in touch and had become close. I'd never forgotten how fierce an advocate she'd been on my behalf.

"Alisa, there's a big victims' rights rally downtown every year. Would you like to be one of our speakers this year?"

My heart beat so hard, I thought it might thump its way right out of my chest. The rights of the victim—this was a cause that was close to me. But to speak publicly would require a degree of exposure I'd never considered.

I'd never said my name out loud before in connection with the trial. Most of my community, even quite a few close friends, didn't know what had happened to me. I hesitated to tell people I met until I'd become close to them, and sometimes I didn't share at all. The rape was no longer the single defining incident of my life, so why bring it up?

When people found out, it often changed the way they were with me. Out came the kid gloves: Suddenly, friends would be falling all over themselves to turn off *Law and Order: SVU* or to apologize for a completely harmless joke.

I could usually get them to forget again—to see me again for loveable old smart-mouthed, sarcastic me—but it still irritated me to be pitied when I'd worked so hard to get to a more empowered place.

So when Susan called, I had to ask myself: Was I ready to come out?

The more I thought about it, the more terrified I became. I was worried that if I spoke out about what I'd gone through, the guys would try to retaliate. But I was more afraid of feeling the way I'd felt at the trials. For weeks, I had dreams where I'd see myself standing up in front of a podium, while people in the audience, their faces contorted with hate and contempt, pointed fingers at me and screamed: "Liar!" "Slut!"

I would wake from those dreams shaking—dry-mouthed, my sheets heavy with my sweat. It was true that I'd come a long way since people had screamed those things at me on my way into the courthouse for the trials. But had I come far enough? How would I feel if nobody believed me? If someone called me a whore or a gold digger? Or told me I'd asked for it, that they hoped I'd learned my lesson, that I'd deserved what happened to me?

I couldn't see what the payoff would be. I'd be putting myself in the line of fire—and for what? I panicked and told Susan I wasn't sure that I'd be able to get the day off from work. That was probably true, but I hadn't asked. I wasn't ready, at that time, to speak.

In the year that followed, though, I daydreamed about what I would say if I ever did have the courage to come forward. I didn't want to dwell on the past or on the gory details of what had happened to me. I am a naturally positive, upbeat kind of person. I have a lot of energy, a sarcastic sense of humor, and an ability to find the silver lining in pretty much any cloud. I imagined my speech being positive, inspirational—maybe even funny at times.

When I pictured giving it, I didn't imagine the audience. Instead, I imagined myself talking to one girl. I couldn't see her face, or anything else about her, but I felt that she was in her late teens and a survivor herself. I kept thinking, "If I can make that one survivor's day a little better, her life a little lighter, with my words, then it's worth it." Daydreaming, I found myself returning over and over to the idea that I could say something to let that girl know that there was an "after," that she wouldn't always feel the way she was feeling.

The next year, in 2012, Susan gave me lots of lead time. "I'd like you to be the main speaker this year," she told me. By then, I was a little more confident in my sobriety and in my faith. Plus, over the course of that year, I'd begun to get more serious about the idea of how I could make my life as meaningful as it could possibly be. When Susan called me again to ask if I would speak, the first thing I thought was: *I've been looking for a way to serve. Could this be it?*

My parents were slightly apprehensive but greatly supportive—if I felt I could do it, they had my back, as always. Shirley thought it was a great idea. "You're ready," she told me. "You have no idea how many people you're going to help." I confessed how much shame I still felt, and she still pushed for me to speak. "Telling your story will help with that, too. You're using what happened to you to do good, and that's going to help you turn this whole nightmare into something you can be proud of."

I prayed on it. I knew that God knew what was best for me, and I tried to open myself up to what He wanted me to do. I asked Him to help me make the decision. I prayed for a long time, sat with the idea that this was a way for me to serve, to use my story and my experiences to help others.

While I was praying, I had a strange thought. *How powerful would it have been, during some of my darkest moments, if I could have received a letter from my future self? What would I write if I knew my younger self could read some inspirational words as I lay shaking on the cold examining table at the hospital, while Tiare held my hand, for instance? Or the day before the second trial, when I was so frightened I thought I was going crazy? What would I say if I could reach back through time and speak to the strung-out self who'd picked the skin on my face to shreds? What would have comforted me on the terrifying nights I spent on that filthy couch behind the McDonald's? How much of a difference would it have made if I had known that it would get better?*

The answer: a lot. It would have meant the world to me. And I realized that I now had the power to do that for someone else. I came away from my prayers believing that speaking out was a way to help, a way for me to explore the calling God had for me.

But I wasn't done praying, not by a long shot. I still had to ask God for the moral courage to stand up in front of hundreds and speak. I opened right up and engaged with Him. I told Him how frightened I was, not only of repercussions from the guys and their families, but also that someone in the audience would accuse me of lying or of having asked for it in some way. I told Him how ashamed I still felt of what happened. I told Him how humiliated I felt by how I'd handled the aftermath, how embarrassed I was to be associated with all the terrible things I'd done. I told Him how naked I would feel, standing up in front of a group of complete strangers and identifying myself as someone who had been raped. I told Him how fragile I felt, how vulnerable and exposed, and I asked Him to be with me.

As I was asking, I realized that I had my answer. God was with me always. He would always know the truth of what had happened to me and the effects it had. And He would give me all the courage I needed, as long as I could ask.

The next day, I called Susan back and said I would do it. I would speak.

There was just one problem: I didn't have any public speaking experience. There's no question that I have what my dad calls the gift of the gab, but with the exception of my experience in rehab, I'd never told my story to more than one or two people at a time. Susan pointed out that they expected hundreds of people at the victims' rights rally. She thought I'd be more comfortable in front of such a huge crowd if I had a little practice.

Susan told me to call Tiare. The rape crisis center that Tiare worked for hosted occasional victim panels, to which they invited people to talk about their experiences in front of the volunteer advocate trainees. Hearing stories from survivors helps brand-new advocates understand the kinds of stories they'll soon be hearing in the field. It teaches them to listen neutrally, without reacting in horror or bursting into tears. It also allows survivors to tell their stories in a completely safe and loving environment, if that's what they need.

Tiare thought it was a terrific idea for me to appear on a victim's panel. I thought it was a terrific idea, too—that is, until the day arrived for me to go there and actually speak. Though I knew it was a smaller group (and one predisposed to be sympathetic), when I was driving over there, I was freaking out. I had never been so nervous in my life. Thank God I was wearing a jacket, because I'd sweat all the way through my blouse by the time I got there.

It was a full house, standing room only. I found out later that a lot of the people in the audience were advocates who had followed my trial closely while it was happening. Of course, nobody had ever heard me say a word, except for my testimony, and they wanted to hear my side of the story.

Another victim spoke first. She'd been abused over a long period by a family member and had very recently come forward. It was hard to listen to; the material was very painful, and she was intensely emotional. It was a good experience for the advocates in training, though, because it was a preview of the kinds of stories they would be hearing when they volunteered. She broke down a few times, unable to go on, and there wasn't a dry eye in the house when she was done.

She was a hard act to follow. But as soon as I started to speak, the nervousness disappeared. As I spoke, I found myself trying to make the tone a little more lighthearted, positive, and inspirational than the previous speaker's tone had been. She was still in it, living through the feelings. By contrast, I'd gained the perspective that comes with time. I went into enough detail to get my point across, but I didn't dwell there. As I was speaking, I realized that the most interesting part about my own story—to me, anyway—was the story of my recovery.

I wanted the advocates to understand how dark and scared and hopeless their clients were feeling, of course. But I also wanted them to feel excited and inspired about their clients' ability to heal and to overcome. It was important to me to tell these helpers that there was hope. I wanted my own sense of optimism and excitement about the future to infect them so that they could bring it to the survivors.

The community at the rape crisis center was, as Susan had predicted, the perfect audience. The other speaker and I got a standing ovation. Everyone was incredibly supportive; I must have hugged seventy strangers that night. The director of the organization at the time gave me a beautiful gift basket she'd put together, and she fastened a handmade bracelet with a teal ribbon and lime-green beads around my wrist. "How did you know that teal is one of my favorite colors?" I asked her. She laughed and told me that teal is the color of National Sexual Assault Awareness month.

"I guess it's meant to be, then," I said.

I felt so elated by how good it had felt to speak that I called my parents on my drive home. It was such a powerful feeling, to see the huge impact I could make simply by telling my story. "I can do this," I told them. "And I think I want to." Any nervousness I might have felt about speaking or about coming out and shedding my Jane Doe status had dissipated completely. Shirley had been right: Coming forward publicly to talk about what had happened to me allowed me to transform a negative, horrible event into something positive.

Rape is about control. The more I talked about what happened to me and determined what the story was, the more control I felt. That night, I was beginning to feel that speaking—as hard as it was for me—was one of the best ways to exercise the calling God had for me. I couldn't wait to do it again.

Still, as the rally approached, I got more and more nervous. There would be hundreds of people there. I'd sweat through my shirt before standing up in front of the most sympathetic audience on earth, the women at Tiare's rape crisis center. How would I feel in front of a giant crowd, when there was no way to guarantee that the audience would be on my side in the same way?

A week before the rally, I had a new, more terrible thought. The rally wasn't specifically for survivors of sexual assault; it was a victims' rights rally. Who knew what horrors the people attending might have lived through? Who knew what tragedies those audience members would be grieving? I knew from Susan that some of the people who'd be in the crowd had lost loved ones to murder or to death by suicide. My own story, as monumentally huge as it loomed in my own life, suddenly seemed piddly and small by comparison. Would those survivors be offended by me thinking that I had anything to offer them? *Did* I have anything to offer them?

I'd pick up the phone to cancel, and then put it down again.

What does a chronic overachiever do when she's nervous? Practice, practice, practice. I must have run through my speech a hundred times. Katie and my poor parents had heard it so often that they knew the darn thing by heart.

Susan warned me that there would be lots of media attention. "There's going to be a ton of press." I thought she was overreacting; after all, it had been ten years. She shook her head. "As soon as you reveal your name, they're going to be coming out of the woodwork. It's going to be a big deal." The first indication that she was right came when she set up some interviews. Journalists swarmed; we accepted only three out of all the requests.

Security was a real concern, so the journalists we did speak to had to agree that they wouldn't publish anything until the day of the rally. Susan went so far as to delay the press release she usually sends out. I'd be accompanied by a team of bodyguards. Still, I could barely hold my head up due to nerves and fear.

The day of the rally, I woke up at the crack of dawn. I dressed carefully, making sure to wear the teal-and-lime-green bracelet that Brenda had given me. Then I prayed.

I prayed all morning. I asked God for courage, for the strength to keep it together. I told God that I didn't care about embarrassing myself, but that I realized I'd been given an opportunity to make a real difference in people's lives, and I didn't want to blow it.

"Please, God, help me to be good enough," I prayed. "Just be with me today."

Susan had been right. It was nuts! There were hundreds of people there, and teams of reporters falling all over themselves to get a picture of me. But the security guys they had there for me were incredibly professional—not to mention gigantic. I let them take care of me, kept my head down, and kept praying until it was my turn to speak.

Just as I had been at the rape crisis center, I was sick with nerves until the moment I stood up to walk over to the podium. As soon as I looked out into the buzzing crowd, all the butterflies in my stomach evaporated, replaced by excitement and a sense of gratitude for the opportunity.

I began to speak, and the words flowed smoothly and freely out of me. I felt invigorated and energized. I felt so strongly about what I was saying that I banged my hand against the podium. (I laughed to see those pictures later.)

One thing that's great about speaking in front of a live audience is the immediate feedback. My parents were there, beaming with pride, as were my grandmother and my aunt. Shirley and Tiare were there, and everyone from the DA's office, and I could see my own triumph on their faces. But strangers were reacting, too. I could see a woman crying in the front row, the faces around her raised expectantly to mine. A guy in the middle pumped his fist when I talked about overcoming. On a couple of occasions, I had to stop to wait for the applause to die down. Another time, I felt a ripple of laughter spread through the crowd because of something I'd said.

There was very little sadness in my speech that day. As far as I was concerned, there'd been enough sadness! It was my goal to stay totally positive and inspiring. I'd always known that I had very specific messages for women who had been raped, as well as for addicts in recovery, but I had tried to make sure that my speech at the rally had more of a general appeal. I wanted to address anybody and everybody going through something they thought they could not survive. I wanted to tell those sufferers that I had myself been to the very depths of hell, but that I had emerged, stronger for the experience. I had wanted to tell every single suffering person who could hear me that they could overcome, and that they would.

At the rally that day, I realized just how far I had come—far enough that I believed I could bring other people along.

I spoke for nine minutes, and for every second of them, I felt I was in exactly the right place at the right time. I had wanted to serve because I believed it would bring me closer to God, and it had: I could feel Him more than ever, right there with me.

...[L]et your light shine before others, that they may see your good deeds and glorify your Father in heaven. (Matthew 5:16, NIV)

When I wrapped up my speech, the people in the audience jumped out of their seats, cheering and applauding. It was the most amazing feeling I'd ever had in my life. Nobody in that audience was accusing me of being a liar or a slut—they were screaming and waving in support.

I spent the rest of the day surrounded by my wonderful security team while people in the audience came up to thank me for my courage and tell me how much my words had helped them. Many of the stories they told me were truly terrible; I went through a whole packet of tissues and borrowed some more from my mom before we were done. But even the people in the very worst part of their experience had taken some positive inspiration from what I had said. I had done it. I had helped.

*   *   *

I believe that in order to rape someone, you have to turn that other person into something less than a person. You have to strip them of their humanity. You have to tell yourself that a drunk, slutty teenager is worth less than your mother or your sister, that she isn't worth anything at all. It's the same mechanism that lets people commit war crimes or traffic in slavery. In order to do these things to another human being, you have to convince yourself that the person you're doing it to isn't human at all.

It's exactly the opposite of the way God sees us, isn't it?

Unfortunately, that dehumanization process doesn't stop with the rape itself. It continues every time someone tells a rape victim not to report what happened to her, every time someone asks what she was wearing, every time she's brutalized by defense attorneys and in the media. It's not surprising that so many victims of rape don't feel very human at all.

That's why standing up at the rally was so important to me. You might not have agreed with everything I said, but hearing me speak, you knew that I was a person. You couldn't dehumanize me or discredit me as nothing more than a dumb teenager who'd made a bad call. I stood up there with dignity and self-respect, able to articulate exactly what had happened to me and everything I'd had to do to find my way to wholeness.

I stood up and spoke for me and for all the women and girls who aren't there yet, those who have accepted their attackers' understanding of them as less than human and have a long way to travel before they can see themselves differently. That was me, for years. Standing up to speak at that rally was a way—almost ten years later—to fight back.

I will never forget that day. It was truly life-changing, one of the most joyful days of my life. I truly felt, standing up there, as if I was doing good work, working to transform the road. It was the work that God had intended for me all along.

## CHAPTER FOURTEEN

# *Struggling Toward Forgiveness*

After the victims' rights rally, I was invited to speak at my aunt Kathy's church.

Speaking there meant I'd be addressing the same women who'd been at the retreat where I'd accepted Jesus into my heart the year before. Her church is about an hour away from my house, and I spent the drive over filled with the spirit and thinking about the year that had passed. It felt very meaningful to me to be speaking there.

That day, I wasn't nervous at all. When I stood up to speak, I felt God with me again. I began, "Hello, my name is Alisa. I'm twenty-six years old. I'm speaking tonight because I'm a survivor of sexual assault. For many years, I was a victim. But today, I'm a survivor, and I owe it all to God. I am amazed by God and His mercy and unconditional love, and I'm going to use the strength and the determination that God has blessed me with to continue to succeed and win, and to help others become survivors, too."

I went on to talk about the blame and shame associated with rape, and about the power of God's love to transform even the most broken life. At the victims' rights rally, I'd been speaking to a secular audience, and I'd wanted my speech to have the widest possible appeal. But it felt great to talk about these issues I cared so much about in a church, to Christians—to testify and to connect the turn-around in my own life with my faith.

The minutes after my speech were filled with tons of hugs and warm wishes. Then Samantha, one of my aunt's friends, approached me. She'd been at the retreat the year before. Like everyone else who'd seen me there in my furious teenager mode, she was astonished by the change in me. We embraced and chatted, and then she asked, "By the way, have you read the passage I highlighted for you yet?"

I had. Before my aunt had given me the pink Bible after that first mountain retreat, a few of her friends had gone through it and marked passages and stories that they especially thought I should read, with little notes in the margins explaining why. Samantha had been one of them. Marking those pages had been a beautiful act of fellowship, and I'd deeply appreciated it. Reading those passages when I got home had helped me to feel that the retreat was ongoing and that I was part of a loving community, although I had not yet found a church of my own. That feeling had sustained me while my mom and I were on our search for a church.

I remembered which passage Samantha had highlighted. "The Joseph story, in Genesis. I did read it! Thank you so much. You were right; there were a lot of important lessons for me there."

"After hearing you speak, I have a feeling you're ready to read it again," Samantha told me. "I'm pretty sure you'll find some new messages in there for you now." I nodded and made a mental note. After all, she'd been right once.

When I got home, one of the first things I did was reread Joseph's story. Joseph is his father's favorite of twelve sons and the recipient of a fantastically colored cloak. His brothers are filled with hatred and jealousy, and they sell him into slavery in Egypt, telling their father that he has been killed. In Egypt, Joseph rises from slavery to become wealthy and powerful, the pharaoh's right-hand man. Then he is wrongly accused of rape and imprisoned. After ten long years in jail, he interprets one of the pharaoh's dreams and rises again.

Because of his leadership, the Egyptians build up their food stores so that there is plenty when famine strikes. Joseph's brothers, meanwhile, have not prepared and are starving. They come to beg for food, not realizing who Joseph has become, although he recognizes them. Instead of turning his brothers away in retaliation for their cruelty, Joseph forgives and feeds them. When his brothers see the forgiveness he's capable of, they tell his father the truth about their actions before he dies.

One of the things I think is so amazing about reading the Bible is how it reflects your own life and concerns back to you, depending on what you're going through. The Joseph story is a good example of this in my own life. When I'd read it the first time Samantha recommended it, after the retreat, the part that resonated with me most strongly was the way that Joseph kept coming back to flourish, though he'd been pushed down over and over and over again. This was someone who did not get beaten down, no matter how hard his trials— someone who went on not just to survive, but to thrive.

That theme still speaks strongly to me, of course. Resilience—the ability to bounce back after encountering adversity—is one of the hottest topics in psychology and education today. But there's no better source for stories about resilience than the Bible. Joshua, Job, Joseph, Naomi, Esther—even Jesus himself. The Bible is filled with people who are tested, often bitterly, and draw upon their faith to get back up and go on, stronger for their struggles.

I was no less interested in resilience than I had been, but Samantha had been right: There were more lessons for me in Joseph's story than the one I had first perceived. Reading the story a year later, I found that it had taken on a whole new dimension. It was as if certain passages were printed in a larger type or had been underlined in bright red pen.

And those passages had to do with forgiveness.


Joseph's story wasn't my first engagement with the concept of forgiveness. I had begun to grapple a little with the idea already. Mostly, though, I'd spent the year coming to terms with the gift of my own forgiveness.

At the retreat, I'd been overwhelmed by the joyful realization that, although I had done some horrible things, I could be forgiven. Over that weekend, I had understood—really understood—that Christ had died so that could happen. Understanding this for the first time drove my decision to stand up and take Jesus into my heart.

What a tremendous gift it was, to be forgiven! For years, I had been consumed by guilt. I felt guilty about the role I'd played in my own rape. I felt guilty about what the aftermath had done to my family, both emotionally and financially. I even felt guilty about pressing charges and ruining the lives of the guys who had assaulted me.

Misplaced or not, this guilt had been my dominant emotion for years, and trying to escape from it had led me down a very dark path. This led to even more guilt, because when I was using drugs, I did a lot of things I wasn't proud of. By the time I had a serious habit, guilt was such an omnipresent feature in my life that those crimes (moral and actual) were simply more fuel for the fire.

Guilt is one of the most toxic emotions we're capable of. Living with a constant, chronic sense of it paralyzes you. It deeply erodes the foundation of your self-esteem and makes you feel completely unlovable. My own sense of guilt and the resulting feeling of worthlessness had been so deep, so complete, that I had tried to kill myself with the drugs.

What a revelation, then, to understand at the retreat what it meant that Jesus had died for us while we were still sinners. He had died so that I might be forgiven! In God's eyes, I wasn't ugly and flawed and destructive and unlovable, but infinitely precious and worthy of redemption. There was no sin too big for Him to forgive; in fact, the only sin He couldn't forgive was the one I didn't bring to Him.

I didn't have to beg for it, either. His love, as I had to remind myself when those guilty feelings marched back in, was unconditional, and His forgiveness was guaranteed. As long as I had repented and turned away from my sins, I could count on that.

To my surprise, the feeling of joy and gratitude that discovering this had given to me didn't wear off. Like most people, I was used to the novelty dulling on anything I was excited about. I'd buy a shirt I couldn't wait to wear, and then a short time later I'd find myself folding it into a bag for Goodwill. Great feelings didn't seem to stick around very long in my life, but the glorious feeling of knowing that God had forgiven me never lessened or felt any less miraculous than it had that night.

That good feeling is one I want to keep going—forever. I never, ever want to go through another notebook like the one I filled doing my fourth step in AA, listing those 112 people I'd hurt and disrespected. I have been forgiven, and I want to stay forgiven. And so, after I started attending church regularly, I began a ritual that I still do every single night before I go to bed. After I've said my evening prayers, I do a mini-fourth step.

I replay my day in my head. If some comment or interaction with someone pops up that I'm not proud of, I need to talk to the person about it. Maybe we need to hash something out together; often, I simply need to apologize. ("I'm sorry I yelled at you when I asked you if my butt looked big in these pants, and you said it sort of did. You were simply telling the truth.") But I need to do something. If I don't address whatever feelings are unresolved, then I'll start to harbor guilt and a lot of bad feelings, and that's not good for me.

I think of it as living clean. You know how people go on cleanses, to detox and get rid of all the garbage that's built up in their systems from eating junk food? My daily inventory helps me to live cleaner, so that there aren't a lot of bad feelings building up and making me sick. Most importantly, it keeps me right with God.

Knowing that I have been forgiven doesn't always mean that I feel forgiven. I still find myself asking, *Is this really it? Isn't there something else I need to do to earn this, to be worthy of this tremendous gift?* It's a gigantic leap of faith to believe in the all-encompassing hugeness of His love. After so many years of feeling unlovable—unlikeable, even—it seems crazy that He can love me. But I know that He does, and with God's help, I've been working toward feeling forgiven—and forgiving myself.


It had not yet occurred to me that my relationships—with God, with other people, and with myself—were also being profoundly affected by the fact that I had not yet taken steps toward forgiving the guys who assaulted me. And it would probably never have occurred to me without church.

At our church, there's a twelve-week class called Wounded Hearts, designed for survivors of trauma and abuse. It was one of the things that had first attracted me to Water of Life, and in 2012 I participated in the group.

It was very powerful to participate, for all the obvious reasons. I had spoken at the victims' rights rally already, but I was in no way done with the shame and blame associated with being a victim of rape. It gave me a lot of comfort to be able to talk about those issues in the company of other Christians who had suffered similarly.

Being in the group was an interesting experience in perspective. When I'd hear another woman blaming herself, it was very easy for me to think, *Cut it out! That's crazy! You didn't do anything wrong!* Even if you're as thickheaded as I am, eventually you have to turn it around: *Oh, right. If she didn't deserve what happened to her, then maybe I didn't deserve what happened to me, either.*

Being in a group of women with similar experiences, especially in a faith-based context, was intensely healing, but it was also very painful. We started the class with thirteen people, and about half of them dropped out, which reminded me of how important it is to be ready to tell your story.

Not everyone is ready to tell their story. First, you have to be ready for the possibility that someone will say something hurtful or upsetting, like "What were you thinking, going to that party by yourself?" There were many years when I was too fragile to hear a comment like that. You also have to be ready for the way attitudes toward you will change. For some people, the fact of your rape will become your primary identity in their eyes. Mostly, you have to come to terms with your own shame and self-hatred around what happened to you, and that can be the hardest part.

I ran into one of the women who had dropped out of our Wounded Hearts group in a hallway at church one Sunday. She dropped her eyes when she saw me and looked as if she wanted to run away. But I stopped her and told her about being in rehab and how long it had taken me to tell the group and my counselors what had happened to me.

"I didn't start getting better until I could tell that story," I told her. "But I wasn't ready to tell it until the moment I told it, and nobody could make me ready to tell it. I had to get there myself. For me, that was an important part of the process. You'll talk about it when you're ready, and when you're ready, I hope that you do."

I had been telling my own story for a while, so speaking that truth wasn't as hard for me as it was for some of the others. I did find it deeply painful to hear the other women's stories, though. Not because the stories were hard to hear—although they were—but because with every one, I was reminded of the terrible toll that rape takes.

What a waste! All these beautiful, strong women, all charged with the difficult work of putting ourselves back together because of someone else's violence. All of us were on a path different from the one we believed we would have taken. All of us struggled with intimacy and relationships. Almost all of us had attempted to anesthetize ourselves, whether through drugs or alcohol or sex or food. Almost all of us had considered suicide at one point or another, and most of us had made an attempt.

Another thing I noticed was how much our extended families had gone through. Some, like my own parents, had suffered terrible stress and financial hardship. Siblings and friends had been neglected. Spouses questioned their own attractiveness. Children struggled with the hardship of living with a depressed parent. The ripple effect was truly profound.

Even as I was marveling over the ways that rape negatively impacts so many of the lives it touches, I felt very proud to be in the company of these amazing women. These were my people, my tribe. These were the survivors. No one should have to get strong in this way, but each of us had gotten stronger at the broken places.

Then, one day, a woman named Emily spoke in that Wounded Hearts class. Hearing her story that day, I first began to grapple seriously with this question of forgiveness.

It certainly wasn't a competition, but no one who attended our class would have denied that Emily's was the hardest story we had heard over the course of the class. She had suffered horrific and systematic abuse at the hands of her parents over a period of twelve years. Hers was the kind of story that makes you think, *I don't want to know this. My understanding of the world is much uglier now that I know that these things take place in it.*

Still, even as the terrible story poured out of her, Emily kept the same sweet demeanor. She wasn't dispassionate and clinical at all, but calm and graceful. She was the only person in the room—including the leader of the group—who wasn't crying.

But it wasn't only her demeanor that impressed me. I listened with disbelief as Emily calmly told us that although her mother continued to lie about being an active participant in the abuse, Emily and her husband made a place for her in their family and in their lives. She told us how blessed she was that she and her husband were able to afford vacations, and she told us about bringing her mother along on some of those trips. That very week, they had bought her mom a new car.

I was shocked. This woman had ruined her life and still Emily was willing to give her the world. After her father's death, she had forgiven him, too, and made periodic trips to visit his gravesite.

What Emily described was completely beyond my comprehension. I saw her peacefulness and grace, and I thought, *Wow. That's what true forgiveness looks like.*

Then I had two more thoughts, pretty much at the same time.

The first was *I want that.*

The second was *And I'm not even close.*

After the class was over, I felt completely wrung out. I could see it in the faces of the others in the group as well; it had taken everything we had to sit there and listen and pray. But I made a special point of approaching Emily, who still seemed completely calm and composed. I thanked her profusely for sharing her story and told her how much I admired her grace and tranquility.

To my surprise, she told me how affecting she'd found my own story, which I'd told the week before. She shook her head. "Honestly, I don't know how you survived what happened to you, or all the stuff that happened afterward. Those trials. A hung jury. Just sickening."

I could hardly believe what she was saying. "Are you serious? You think that what I went through was bad, when you endured twelve years of the worst kind of abuse—and at the hands of your parents, the people who were supposed to dedicate their lives to loving and taking care of you?"

I shared with her how impressed I was by her ability to forgive, and I told her I didn't think I'd ever be able to get to where she was. Emily didn't try to talk me out of my position, but before we parted ways, she said, "You don't forgive them for them—your abusers. You forgive them so that you can move on with your life."

Long after the class was over, I found myself returning over and over to Emily's words. I found I was thinking about forgiveness more seriously than I ever had in the past.

It occurred to me that God seemed to have been putting

other stories about forgiveness in my path. Driving home one afternoon, for instance, about six months before I'd met Emily, I'd heard someone tell a story on the radio about a man—a pastor—whose son had been murdered in a bar fight. He developed a relationship with the young man who'd killed his son while the young man was in jail, a relationship that developed over the years from casual to more intimate. They became as close as a father and son; in fact, when his son's killer was released and got married, the pastor performed the ceremony.

When I'd heard that story (and I sat in my driveway so I could hear the end), I thought: *I'm sorry, but that is completely nuts.* I couldn't wrap my brain around the idea, couldn't imagine feeling that way. I thought about how much space that pastor must have in his heart, how much compassion and empathy and generosity, and I knew, without a shade of doubt, that I didn't have that much love.

But I couldn't get the story out of my head, either. It would pop up at the weirdest moments—when I was driving to work, or doing crunches at the gym, or feeding my parents' dogs.

Then I remembered that in 2006, a man entered a one-room schoolhouse in Pennsylvania with a gun and killed ten girls, aged six to thirteen, and then himself. That very day, mere hours after the shooting, the Amish community extended forgiveness to the family of the shooter. They met with his widow, invited her to one of the girls' funerals, and held the killer's father while he wept. Members of that community went so far as to set up a charitable foundation for his family. I was using drugs then, and so I was pretty much oblivious to everything going on in the world around me, but I had followed the story of what had happened in that Amish schoolhouse closely while it was happening. Why had I been so interested in this story about the incredible capacity of a community to forgive?

Then, at the Wounded Hearts group, I had heard Emily's story. It was a story I could relate to, but that was from a perspective much worse than my own. More than anything, I kept thinking about how soft and sweet she'd seemed, how peaceful. I felt a lot of admiration for the open, honest way she'd told her story. There was nothing twisted about her, nothing hard or hateful. And so it was that I found myself wondering if could I forgive my own abusers.

At one level, it seemed completely impossible. On the other hand, when Jesus was dying on the cross, he said, "Father, forgive them, for they know not what they do." And that was while his murderers were gambling for his clothes! If He could forgive them, who was I to harden my heart?

I already had the slightest taste of what it might mean to forgive. Just a few months after my rape, one of the therapists I'd seen had encouraged me to write letters addressed to my attackers. We would never send them; they'd never see what I'd written. This was just for me.

The therapist asked me, "If you could say anything in the world you wanted to, what would you say?"

When I sat down to write to Seth and Jared, I spewed

pure bile; there was nothing in there but white-hot anger, seasoned with a little hate and a few choice curse words.

But my letter to Brian was a little different. I asked him, "Why didn't you protect me? You were my boyfriend. I thought we really liked each other." I let all of my confusion and hurt out onto the page. I wrote:

I'm so sorry that you gave into that peer pressure. Unfortunately, it changed our lives forever, and not for the better. But I see now that it was a mistake—a terrible, disgusting mistake—but a mistake all the same. It was so wrong, but ultimately it was a horrible, horrible, decision, one that had horrible repercussions on all of us, and will for the rest of our lives.

It was incredibly intense to write like that, to dump every single thing I was thinking and feeling onto the page without any self-consciousness or conflict at all. I was genuinely shocked at where I'd ended up. I thought I'd vomit every hateful four-letter word in my vocabulary onto the page, and then I'd make some new ones up. Instead, I found that I felt very compassionate toward Brian. I had ended up very close to a place of forgiveness, at least where he was concerned.

Without realizing it, I had experienced why Christians say that forgiveness can be transformational. The strangest thing happened after I wrote that letter: I felt lighter somehow. It was so surprising, I even mentioned it to the therapist. But I'm pretty sure I would have laughed in her face (and stormed out of her office) if she'd implied that the lightness was somehow connected to my ability to forgive.

By the time I met Emily, I was ready for the lesson. I was finally able to recognize that sense of lightness for what it was: freedom. That was the reason that story about the pastor, who became a father figure to the man who had murdered his son, had stuck with me, though I couldn't understand it. The pastor and Emily were free in a way that I was not, and their ability to forgive was the key.

Someone once sent me a Mark Twain quote: "Anger is an acid that can do more harm to the vessel in which it is stored than to anything on which it is poured." There's a physical aspect to that image that spoke to me: I pictured a metal oil drum, rusted out and corroded at the bottom. I was filled with rage for years, and that was the way it felt, too, as if there were a bowlful of vile and dangerous liquid sloshing around in my guts, ready to spill over and burn a toxic hole with the slightest jostle.

I had to ask myself: Did I want to spend the rest of my life hanging on to the anger I felt toward those guys? Did I want to become ugly—corroded and broken—in my resentment? Was that what I wanted to be reflecting back into the world and to everyone I had relationships with? Hating them the way I did kept me shackled to them. It tied our lives together in a way that was openly hurtful to me, as if I'd never gotten up off that pool table. Was that truly where I wanted to spend the rest of my life?

The answer, of course, was no. I tried feeling bitter and cynical and hopeless, and it didn't work for me. Not only did it feel terrible and lead me to make a lot of pretty terrible decisions, but it wasn't me. I'm a sunny, optimistic person at heart. I love to wear bright colors and giggle and be silly. I want to love and be loved in my life. Thanks to my volunteering, I'd had a glorious taste of what it means to help, to feel useful and necessary, doing God's work. That was where I wanted to stay: in the light. I wrote in my journal:

> *I don't want to spend my entire life angry about the way it was hijacked when I was sixteen. I want to live my fullest, most joyful life.*

After I met Emily, I finally understood that I wouldn't be able to do that until I'd learned what Jesus taught us, that all of us deserve to be forgiven.

W anting to forgive is one thing.

The reality of trying to actually do it? That's a different story.

Crazily enough, I'm afraid to write that. I'm afraid of disappointing my readers. But it's the truth. If you came to this book looking for a done deal—a woman who can look her abusers in the eyes with nothing but compassion and God's love in her heart, then I'm truly, genuinely sorry, because I am simply not there yet. I'm a lot closer than I was ten years ago, and I get closer every day. But I can't pretend that this forgiveness issue is closed for me, because that wouldn't be the truth, and the one rule I have for myself now is that I will always do my very best to tell the truth.

And the truth is that forgiving is hard. It's turning out to be some of the hardest work I've ever done—harder, for sure, than getting clean or making amends. My path toward forgiveness has been a daily and mighty struggle.

It's also the most important thing I'm trying to do in my life. I believe in its power—for myself and for other survivors. But I will not (and couldn't, if I tried) pretend that it has been easy for me.

For sure, it's gotten better. At the beginning of this journey, I'd pray on forgiveness, and I'd find myself getting mad all over again. How could these men—people I thought I knew and could trust—abuse me the way that they had? I'd think about Susan Schroeder, who has spent her entire career dealing with violent crime, and what she said after seeing the video: "It really makes you question your basic assumptions about humanity." I'd think about how cowardly the guys were to take advantage of me while I was unconscious. Of course, it still wouldn't have been a fair fight if I'd been awake—I weighed about 120 pounds, and there were three of them—but at least I'd have had the satisfaction of knowing that I tried to fight back.

Then I'd start thinking about the way my life had been derailed. Would I have become a drug addict living with a succession of abusive boyfriends if I hadn't been raped? Nobody has a crystal ball, but I don't think so. I'd compare where I thought I'd be—a glamorous journalist in New York City—with my reality: broke and struggling through college, years older than everyone else in my classes. Then I'd start thinking about how far behind I'd fallen in other areas of my life as well. My peers were getting married and starting families, while my own problems with intimacy made it hard for anyone I was dating to get past the glittery, hard surface I presented them with.

And so it would go—on and on and on. I'd start trying to work on forgiveness, and I'd end up delivering a tired litany to myself on all the ways the guys had ruined my life. It was hardly the place of peace and compassion I was aiming for! I knew what I wanted to do—what I needed to do, in order to move on. Why, then, couldn't I do it?

And then I'd end up getting angry all over again—this time, at myself.

The quote I found that helped me the most was from the death penalty activist Sister Helen Prejean, a Roman Catholic nun who counsels men waiting for execution and founded an organization dedicated to the families of the victims of violent crime. She once said, "Forgiveness isn't something that happens. It's something you pray for and struggle toward, every single day."

When I read that, I let out a little sigh of relief. You'd think knowing that would make it harder, but the idea of forgiveness as a process eased the pressure a little and still does, especially on those days when it seems completely out of my reach. Reading that quote, I understood that forgiveness wasn't an item I'd be able to scratch off my to-do list. This was something I would spend a lifetime grappling with.

If I had to describe where I am in terms of forgiveness right now, I'd say that some days are better than others. I'm making progress, but it's not easy. I read a lot about the topic, I talk a lot about it with other Christians, and I pray a lot.

So if you were someone who was drawn to this book because you thought there might be some guidance toward achieving forgiveness in these pages, the best I can do is share the insights I've picked up on this difficult path. These are the ideas that I find myself returning to, over and over.

The first thing I always ask when I find myself holding a hard heart is a very simple question: *Am I living as Jesus would? Where in my life do I need to be more like Him?*

Right away, that causes me to soften a little. I don't know much, but I know that Jesus didn't harden His heart or give in to hatred and judgment. And when I think about what He went through on the cross, I can't feel anything but gratitude.

I also try to remember that forgiveness is what allows me to see the defendants in my case as people. As I've already said, I believe dehumanization is behind most of the terrible things we do to one another. I've been dehumanized myself—first on that pool table, and again in the courtroom and in the press. And I don't want any part of doing it to someone else—even to the people who did it to me.

The guys who sexually assaulted me made a sequence of terrible mistakes, mistakes that derailed all of our lives, and many others, too. But they're not animals or aliens—they're people, just like you and me.

I think this is an important point, not just in my particular case, but when we're thinking about healing the road to Jericho, too. It's tempting (and very dangerous) to categorize men and boys who rape as animals. Too often, when we read about a rape case, our tendency is to dismiss the perpetrators as sociopaths. "Who are these sickos?" we ask ourselves. But the truth is that most of the men who rape aren't lunatics or sick aberrations, but brothers, sons, boyfriends, husbands—participants in a society that does little to discourage rape. We will never stop rape until we acknowledge this.

So I try to remind myself, when I am struggling to forgive, that it's the right thing to do, the thing that Jesus would have done. I also feel a moral imperative to do it, because it forces me to acknowledge the men who attacked and abused me as people. But the thing that helps me most in my struggle toward forgiveness is the realization that a refusal to forgive gets in the way of my relationship with God.

I also often reread the story in Matthew in which a servant is forgiven a major debt but then fails to forgive someone else who owes him a little money. The king orders the servant to be tortured until he has paid everything he owes back, and Jesus says,

This is how my heavenly Father will treat each of you unless you forgive your brother or sister from your heart. (Matthew 18:35, NIV)

When I'm struggling, it helps me to remember that I myself have been forgiven. It took me a long time to connect the fact that I have been forgiven with the act of forgiving my attackers. Now that I've seen it, though, I can't deny that the connection is there. When we say the Lord's Prayer, we say, "forgive us our sins, for we also forgive everyone who sins against us" (Luke 11:4, NIV). I believe that there's a reason we ask for forgiveness for ourselves first. Whatever compassion I have stems from knowing that I myself have been forgiven an enormous debt, one I never have expected to be forgiven. It is my responsibility, my part of that covenant, to share that forgiveness with others.

I want to allow for the possibility that the guys might themselves experience the feeling of being forgiven, although I'll never know if they do. I do hope and pray every day that they can forgive themselves, though. If there's one thing I know from my own experience, it's that if they don't forgive themselves, they're never going to be happy.

The other thing that has really helped me is returning to the Joseph story. I try to put myself in his shoes. When Joseph was in jail all those years, did he dwell in hatred? I'd certainly understand if he did. Did he think about revenge? Did he fantasize about all the ways his life would have been different if he'd never been sold into slavery? The Bible doesn't tell us, but there's a very revealing passage a little later. When Joseph reveals himself to his brothers later, he tells them not to be afraid. He explains that they shouldn't feel bad for what they've done, because of all the lives he's saved by being in Egypt.

> And now, do not be distressed and do not be angry with yourselves for selling me here, because it was to save lives that God sent me ahead of you. For two years now there has been famine in the land, and for the next five years there will be no plowing and reaping. But God sent me ahead of you to preserve for you a remnant on earth and to save your lives by a great deliverance. So then, it was not you who sent me here, but God. He made me father to Pharaoh, lord of his entire household and ruler of all Egypt. (Genesis 45:5–8, NIV)

He says that God sent him ahead. In other words, he has risen above the pain by finding meaning in what happened to him, by trusting that God had a big-picture reason for all the pain and suffering He put Joseph through.

That is what I am trying to do, too.

Over the years, it's helped me a lot to isolate what forgiveness is from what it isn't.

I know now that forgiveness doesn't mean apologizing for my attackers or letting them off the hook for what they did. It doesn't mean that I was wrong to seek justice in the courts. It doesn't mean that I fully understand how they could do what they did, or that I ever will. It definitely doesn't mean condoning their actions.

Forgiving them doesn't even have to mean that I feel particularly forgiving. But I choose to forgive them anyway. Forgiveness is in the choosing.

Another thing about forgiving: It doesn't mean forgetting. I've tried to explain this to my dad many times, as he has a harder time separating the two. What those guys did is a part of me, a part of who I am. Not a day goes by when I don't think about it in some way, and I'm pretty sure that'll be true for the rest of my life. So there's no question about forgetting. But as much as the rape is a part of my story, it's by no means the whole story. I know that, and so does God.

Forgiveness certainly doesn't mean reconciliation. If this were the movie version of my life, maybe the final scene would be a long shot through a window, showing the four of us sitting down around a table and breaking bread together. But this isn't a movie, and the thought of seeing one of them makes me feel nauseated. If I ran into one of them at the grocery store, I'm pretty sure I'd just flee. I think about the story of the pastor who was able to bless his son's killer and have that person in his life, and I'm not sure I'll ever get there—or that such a thing is even a worthwhile goal for me.

So how far have I gotten on this long and torturous path toward—hopefully, eventually—forgiving the men who assaulted me? I want to forgive them, I have chosen to forgive them, and I am working on it, every day—one at a time.

I can tell you that I pray every day of my life for them.

I pray that they have been able to go on and live happy lives—that they have work that fulfills them, a community that nurtures them, and relationships that sustain them. They did a terrible thing, but they have paid for it, and they deserve to be happy now. Everybody does.

And when I do achieve forgiveness—even for a moment, a split second—I know it's a miracle. Left to my own devices, I cannot forgive. It's only with God's help that I can feel it.

## CHAPTER FIFTEEN

# A Final Step

You go your entire life without thinking about something—and then suddenly you can't get away from it. Without any prompting from you, it crops up in every conversation, every television commercial, every magazine article you're flipping through while you're waiting for your manicure to dry.

That's how it was for me, with baptism.

Before I joined our church, I'd never thought about baptism. When I joined Water of Life, I didn't even know what it was. I thought it was something that could only happen when you were a baby. There wasn't a lot of talk about it at church, either; our church doesn't push baptism at all. It's something they feel you should come to of your own volition, and I profoundly agree with this, because of the way I saw it happen for me. Baptism wasn't a natural next step, but something I had to work for—something I had to research, and learn about, and come to desire with all my heart.

I believe that you hear about the things you need to hear about right when you need to hear about them—and there's no question in my mind that God was putting the idea of baptism in my path. Because, about a year after the retreat in the mountains, I found the topic coming up constantly.

I'd been going to church for a year or so, and I'd learned more about baptism than I ever knew growing up. The first occasion I had to wrestle with the concept of baptism came one morning during my Bible reading. I ran across this passage:

> So in Christ Jesus you are all children of God through faith, for all of you who were baptized into Christ have clothed yourselves with Christ. (Galatians 3:26–27, NIV)

*Clothed with Christ.* That metaphor made instant sense to me. In fact, I ran my highlighter over the passage so many times I thought I'd wear straight through the page. I called my mom to read it to her because I knew she'd understand: This quote was just the way I felt since I'd taken Christ into my heart.

But as my mom's line was ringing, I reread the quote and realized that, in my enthusiasm, I'd skipped something important my first read through—I hadn't been baptized. As close to Him as I felt, there was still a crucial step missing, a step pointed to in the passage itself: I couldn't be clothed with Christ because I hadn't been baptized into Him. I slowly put down the phone, before my mom had even picked up.

That morning was the beginning of a journey for me. I started to investigate baptism, what it meant and why people of faith did it. And the more I learned, the more I started to feel the importance of this missing step.

One of the things that appealed to me about baptism was the public nature of the commitment. Maybe it was because I'm such a private person, but I knew how important it can be to make a public declaration of your intention. Standing up and admitting that I was an addict had been a powerful step in my recovery. Telling my group in rehab about the rape had been an essential step in beginning to shed my own shame around what had happened to me and had played a huge part in my being able to move on. It had been deeply meaningful to me to stand up and proclaim my faith at that retreat in the mountains. This wasn't just a revelation I was having in the privacy of my own living room; it meant something to say it out loud, to people I knew and to strangers.

The same thing applied to baptism. Jesus had been baptized in the river Jordan, in front of everyone. I felt ready to go public, too. I wanted to proclaim my faith; I wanted to join the larger family of God. And the more I came to value my church community at Water of Life, the more I wanted to profess my faith there, so that I could be formally accepted into the fold.

Mostly, though, I wanted to celebrate and make official

the internal change in me. As I became more and more excited about the changes my faith was making possible in my life, the more I wanted to celebrate it. I wanted to "put on" Christ, to be united with Him through baptism. I'd been dipping my toe—wasn't it time to take the plunge?

After about a year of asking questions and reading everything I could get my hands on, I came to a realization: I wanted to be baptized. But there was a tether holding me back, and it was a strong one: my relationship with my father.

My newfound faith hadn't been easy for my dad to accept. Although he doesn't actively practice his Judaism, he does feel strongly, ethnically Jewish. His own grandfather was a survivor of the concentration camps, as the number tattooed on his wrist reminded him every day.

Nor is my father's faith totally dormant. He doesn't read the Bible or go to temple or celebrate Jewish holidays. But, unbeknownst to me, he had turned to a rabbi for comfort, support, and counseling during the worst parts of the two trials. Their conversations had given him some relief when he'd felt deeply vulnerable and isolated.

So it had nearly broken his heart to see me walk away from his family's culture. He felt his Judaism was going to end with him, and that was deeply painful for him. My growing faith also caused a lot of tension between him and my mother, because she'd been such an integral part of me discovering who I was as a Christian.

My dad never came right out and told me how miserable it made him to see me going to church. Obviously, he felt very conflicted. You'd have to be blind not to see how good it had been for me to find faith. I was clean, strong, and healthy. I was living on my own, holding down a good job, and back at school. All of these things would have seemed completely out of the realm of possibility a few years before. Maybe most importantly, I laughed easily again.

So my father could see exactly how much stronger and happier my faith had made me, but he couldn't give the credit where it was due. He'd say, "Alisa, I'm so proud that you've been able to turn your life around. But that was you! You did that—because you're a fighter, because you're strong, because you refused to give up."

All I could do was shake my head. Couldn't he see that it had also been "just me" using meth in a house where kids were living? Or relapsing and lying about it to everyone, even myself? I'd love to take all the credit for my miraculous recovery. But I knew all too well that, alone, I hadn't been able to turn my life around—not until I'd asked for the right kind of help.

The tension building in our family over the issue of my faith generally simmered under the surface, but I knew that if I told my dad I wanted to be baptized, it would blow the issue wide open.

And I wasn't at all sure that I could handle that. Most of us want to make our parents happy, especially if we had a happy childhood. Because of my circumstances, though, I felt more strongly motivated than most. My dad has been there for me, every step of the way. He was there, riding his bike next to me while I was training for my cross-country races, feeding me jokes and the inspiration I needed to keep going. He gave me nothing but strength and support during the aftermath of my rape and during the trials, and I can never repay him for the constancy of his love when I was struggling with my meth addiction. I still felt very guilty about how much stress I had brought into my parents' lives and marriage between the trials and my drug use.

Now that I was healthy and back on track, I wanted more than anything to be a source of pride and love and fun for my parents, the way it always should have been. And in the years that followed my getting off drugs, that dream had seemed possible. Being able to share my spiritual life with my mother had proven to be more richly rewarding than I could have imagined. Every time we went to church together or held hands in prayer, I felt like I was applying a healing salve to a relationship that had been damaged almost beyond repair.

But now that same agent of healing seemed to be driving a painful wedge between me and my father. I just couldn't believe that the wedge was God and church—without question, the most positive things in my life! And yet, as my faith deepened and my commitment grew, I couldn't avoid the truth: My belief was becoming a wedge.

I'd always loved the long philosophical discussions I'd had with my dad. We'd ramble over every topic under the sun, from music to movies to politics, laughing and quarreling. But as my thinking became more influenced by what I was reading in the Bible and what I was hearing during the sermon on Sunday mornings, I was finding that our conversations didn't flow as easily anymore. As soon as I mentioned anything to do with Christianity, my dad would shut down. If he came over to my condo to fix a leaky tap or to drop some clothes off from my mom, I could see how hard he had to work to ignore the angels in my bedroom and the Bible quotes on my walls. It was as if he took them personally, a targeted insult directed at him and at his heritage.

Mostly, we didn't talk about it all that much. But we did butt heads, particularly around the idea of forgiveness.

My dad and I argue all the time—that's what happens when two bullheaded, stubborn lunatics end up in the same family. We'll quarrel about the best route to avoid traffic, the right place to park, what we should pick up for dinner, the best James Bond. But we can usually appreciate the other person's position—even when we're both completely convinced that the other person is totally, completely, unbelievably wrong.

That had been true my whole life, and it was still true—except when we were talking about forgiveness. On this one topic, we were missing each other completely, fundamentally unable to relate to one another, as if we were speaking different languages.

Our conversations always went the same way.

"How can you even begin to think about forgiving those animals?" my dad would ask me, incredulous. And no matter how many times I explained to him what living in a

236

constant state of unresolved anger had been doing to me and how much more free I'd felt since I'd started to work toward something different, he couldn't move off the X. I could see that he wasn't just being a pain about it—he genuinely didn't understand. He'd look at me as if I'd been brainwashed.

He wasn't the only one who was freaked out by the other person's position. The level of anger and hate my dad still held in his heart began to make me deeply uncomfortable. I could see what that kind of rage looked like in a way that I hadn't understood before, and how toxic an effect it had on the person holding it. Lewis B. Smedes, who wrote a great book about forgiveness called *Forgive and Forget: Healing the Hurts We Don't Deserve*, says, "To forgive is to set a prisoner free and discover that the prisoner was you." It seemed to me my dad was serving life without parole.

"Why stop with the guys?" I asked him once, when we were debating the issue. I was trying to push him, so he could see how absurd his attitude was. "Why not go ahead and hate all the lawyers, and the private investigators, and the friends who deserted me, and all the people who lined up outside the courtroom so they could call me a slut, and everyone who said I deserved what happened to me in the comments section of every random newspaper article about the trials?"

He stared at me as if I were an alien.

"But I do," he said simply.

That really frightened me. I'd been exaggerating so he could see how crazy it was to hold that level of hatred in his heart. Clearly, I'd misunderstood the parameters of his rage.

It made me feel so sad for him. Where would that fury end? And how could there be any room for anything more positive and healing in his heart when it was filled to the brim with poison? Forgiveness might not be a done deal for me, but working toward it had opened my life right up. I could laugh easily again. I was taking responsibility for my own life. Now that I'd seen how the world could be when I greeted it with more compassion and less anger, I wanted a sweeter, happier worldview for my dad, too.

In fairness, I didn't ever feel that my faith was threatened by my father's refusal to get on board with it. But the growing rift between us wounded me deeply.

My relationship with him meant everything to me. The idea that I could disappoint him in such a huge way made me feel physically sick—especially because the defining factor of our relationship as I saw it was that he'd never, ever let me down. At the same time, I knew that I had found my own truth, a truth that supported my sobriety and was key to living the life I wanted to live. And I wished, for his sake, that he could find some of the peace and comfort that I'd found from my faith.

I'd hit an impasse. With all my heart, I wanted to pursue baptism, and yet I knew that to do so would break my father's heart.

The tension became unbearable. The more committed I

felt to God and the church, the more my sense of urgency around the issue of my baptism grew. As far as I understand it, baptism is the final step in opening your life to Him, the signal that your acceptance of Him is complete. The more I learned and read, the more sure I became that it was something I desperately wanted to do.

This was especially true because of what had happened to me. Baptism has a special resonance for trauma survivors. In Romans it says,

> Or don't you know that all of us who were baptized into Christ Jesus were baptized into his death? We were therefore buried with him through baptism into death in order that, just as Christ was raised from the dead through the glory of the Father, we too may live a new life. (Romans 6:3–4, NIV)

Those words were so powerful to me. I thought of myself as someone celebrating a brand-new life. I had been forgiven, and so much had changed. As part of my new life, I wanted to bury the old one, to be able to say without qualification that I had turned away from sin and the poor decisions born out of my trauma and from living away from God. I wanted to live a Christian life, a life I didn't have to be ashamed of. I wanted to be washed of my sins, as Peter wrote I would be, and to start my new life walking with Him.

I sat with the baptism decision for almost two years. I talked to other Christians whose families did not fully understand their devotion. That helped me. And I prayed on it, a lot.

Over that time, I found myself thinking about all the occasions on which the darker path had beckoned me. For instance, some months after the retreat in the mountains, when I was cleaning out some drawers in my childhood bedroom so my parents could use the room, I came upon a baggie of meth that I'd hidden there when I was still using. I held that bag in my hands, and the compulsion to do it was stronger than almost any feeling I had ever had. It would have been so easy to lay out a line and fall again into that blessed oblivion. But then I heard someone start to scream. It was a terrible, high-pitched scream, as if someone were being murdered, but I had no idea where it was coming from. My parents rushed into the room. They grabbed me and held me, but all I could do was hold the bag of meth out in front of me, pushing it into my dad's hands. "Hush, hush," my mom said, holding me tight. It was then that I realized that the screaming was coming from me. Thinking about that story later, I knew that God and Satan had both been in that room. It had been my faith that had saved me.

A couple of months after that, a friend from my drug days called me. I hadn't heard from him for years, but I could tell as soon as I heard his voice that he was high. Apparently, he was also a fugitive: He'd been arrested and hadn't checked in for his court date. This was someone who had been important to me when I was using. We'd been very close, and when he begged me to let him crash at my condo, I strongly felt the urge to help. What could it hurt? I wasn't going to use. Maybe I could help him to get clean. Then I heard the truth, as if someone—God again—had spoken it aloud. My friend wasn't anywhere close to being ready to get clean, and my sobriety, as secure as it may have been, would not have benefited from the drama of having an active drug user living in my home. "I love you," I said, "and I want to help. But I can't have drugs around me, and I can't harbor a fugitive in my home. When you're ready to get clean, give me a call." It was the right thing to do and a reminder that if I listen to Him, He'll always point the way.

The more I read and learned, the more baptism started to feel less like a choice and more like an imperative. Jesus gave us the sacraments to remind us of his death and resurrection, and they aren't presented as suggestions, but as commands. Baptism is a surrender, a sign of our obedience to God. I put this quote from Proverbs on my wall:

> Trust in the LORD with all your heart and lean not on your own understanding; in all your ways submit to him, and he will make your paths straight. (Proverbs 3:5–7, NIV)

Over and over, I had seen the wisdom of those words proven to me. Leaning on my own understanding had led me astray, time and time again. Whenever I felt hopeless about how much less I knew than people who had been raised in the church, all I had to do was read that quote, and I could breathe again. The passage was clear: All I needed to do was submit.

But what if submitting meant devastating one of the people closest to me?

It took lots of prayer, but ultimately I knew what I had to do. I came to realize that I couldn't play both sides of the field anymore. I wanted to commit myself fully to God.

To do that, I would have to take a stand.

It helped me to know, through prayer, that my motives were true. My decision to get baptized wasn't a childish rebellion against my dad, a way to thumb my nose at his values, but an affirmation of everything that had been positively and powerfully transformative in my life. I would ask for his blessing. If he gave it to me, it would be the happiest day of my life. If not, though, I would go ahead anyway. It wasn't a personal attack against him. I needed to do this for me.

I asked my dad to meet me for lunch, as I often did. We went to an Italian restaurant near my work. I was so nervous, I could hardly concentrate on the menu. Finally, I blurted it out.

"Daddy, I've got news to tell you. I'm going to get baptized."

There was an alarmingly long pause, and then he said, "Obviously, I don't agree with the decision. But it's your choice, and you've chosen."

We pushed the pasta around our plates in silence for a while, and then my dad asked me, "What does it mean, to be baptized?"

Surprised, I told him that baptism meant turning my life over to God, it meant committing 100 percent to Him and to a life I didn't have to be ashamed of. I told him how important it was to me to take this final step. He nodded, as if absorbing what I'd told him. Then he asked another question, and then another, as if he was testing me. What did baptism mean in the Bible? Why had I waited so long? Would it change the way I lived?

I answered his questions as best I could, thrilled he was engaging with me on the topic at all. It was clear he wasn't thrilled about it, but neither was he directly challenging my decision. It was more than I'd hoped for but less than I'd dreamed of. Was it completely unrealistic to hope for his support?

I'd been talking to my mother about baptism the two years I'd been thinking and praying and searching. She'd deliberately taken a neutral position. Better than anyone, she understood that I didn't want to upset my father; by the same token, she could see how much making the commitment was beginning to mean to me.

She'd understood how important it was for me to make the decision to be baptized on my own, with no interference or outside influence. So during our many conversations about my desire to take this final step, my mom mostly asked questions and listened to my answers. The only advice she gave me was to keep praying about it. "Keep talking to God," she told me. "He'll make the answer clear." It was good advice. I had, and He had.

A lot of those conversations with my mom took place in the front seat of her car. Every Sunday, she drives over to my house and picks me up so we can take her car to church.

After the drive home, we sit in my driveway—often for an hour or more—and talk. The conversation is free-ranging, covering everything from what we're going to wear for the holidays to the big-picture issues of life and love and faith. Some of our best conversations have happened in the front seat of that car, so it felt fitting that it was where I finally told my mom that I'd made the decision: I was going to be baptized at Water of Life.

There's a mandatory class that you have to take in order to be baptized at Water of Life. I'd registered already, and the class was starting soon. And I was nursing a secret, private hope that my mom would join me.

I'd gone online to register for the class, and one of the questions on the registration form was "Is this the first time you have been baptized, or are you having a rebaptism?" Underneath, it explained that a rebaptism is for those who had been baptized before but who had stopped living a Christian life for one reason or another. When those people came back to church and felt that they wanted to give their lives back to God, they could be rebaptized.

The paragraph couldn't have jumped out at me more if it had been surrounded by blinking lights. My mom had been baptized as a young girl. But she had spent the majority of her adult life living away from the church. As soon as I read the question about rebaptism, I knew that it described my mom's situation exactly.

In the time that we'd been going to church, my mom had her faith restored to her, as she put it. It made me think of a beautiful old piece of furniture, broken and forgotten in the back of someone's garage, dried out and covered with layers of grime and dust, until finally someone comes along who can recognize how beautiful the piece is, someone willing to invest the labor and patience to make it whole again. The next time you see it, that piece of furniture has been transformed by love. It's sturdy again, polished to a gleam with beeswax, and restored to its former glory.

I had that idea of restoration in my head when I told my mom about my decision to be baptized, and I asked her if she'd consider doing it with me.

"Mom," I started, not sure what she'd think. "I'm going to take the class. And I'd really love you to come, too."

Then I explained everything I'd learned about rebaptism, and how perfectly I felt it described her own situation. She was incredibly excited about the opportunity and quickly said yes. My mom wanted a new life, too, and to celebrate the restoration of her faith. She hadn't realized it was an option, either.

She only had one hesitation: She didn't want to horn in on my big day.

"I know how enormous a step this is for you, Alisa," she told me. "Don't you want the attention to be on you?"

I told her the truth, which was that I couldn't imagine anything more perfect than sharing my day with her. We hugged and cried a little, and both agreed that I'd sign her up for the class, too. I was thrilled we'd be doing it together.

A week later, after dinner at their house, we were all

watching TV together, and I paused the show. "Dad, I'm getting baptized next week, and I hope you'll be there. I completely understand if you don't feel you want to attend, and I promise I won't be mad if you decide not to. But if you could be there, it would mean the world to me."

He didn't say anything for a while, but just sat there in his recliner with his hands pressed together, his toes tapping together the way they do when he's mad. We sat there in silence, my own hands pressed into my lap so I didn't have to see them shake.

Finally he said, "I've always supported you in something positive, Alisa." It was true—he had. "I may not like this, but I've always loved you. I'll be there."

I couldn't contain myself—first I started crying, and then I jumped onto his lap.


In the week leading up to my baptism, I was a little kid waiting for Christmas.

Unfortunately, the day would not turn out to be everything I had expected.

Not at all, in fact.

The morning got off to a bad start. I overslept, and so I had to rush through my morning routine to get to the church on time. I like my personal appearance to be just so, and I wasn't thrilled with having to throw myself together in a rush on one of the most important days of my life.

I noticed how chilly it was as soon as I opened the door to my house, but of course it was too late to change. "I'll stand in the sun," I thought, rubbing my arms for warmth. I'm a California girl, used to 75 degrees and sunny. And in Southern California, 75 degrees and sunny is almost always what you get.

Not the day of my baptism. By the time we got to the shallow pool where the baptism would take place, it wasn't cold—it was freezing. My mom had had the foresight to grab a cardigan, but I was in a short-sleeved dress and openly shivering. The sky was overcast, so there was no sun to stand in. The cold was one thing, but it was made drastically worse by a gale-force wind, the kind of wind you have to put your head down and brace yourself to walk into. The palm trees near the baptism pool were bending over so dramatically, I was worried they were going to break in half.

I was pleased to see that my dad was there in the audience, but there was very little warmth coming off him. In fact, I could see that he was in a full-on bad mood—what my mom and I called crankypants mode. Watching him in the crowd and seeing that sour look on his face reminded me of myself the first night at the retreat in the mountains. I pitied whomever he was standing next to.

The wind was so bad that the guys manning the snack bar tent near the pool packed up their wares and went inside. They were so desperate to get inside that they gave away everything they'd been selling. My dad scored two free donuts, which was probably the best thing that happened to him that whole day.

That wind meant we couldn't hear a thing the pastor was saying; the words got ripped right out of the pastor's mouth as soon as he opened it. It also meant that the videographer had to go inside.

That there would be no video was especially upsetting to me. It might sound silly, but I was looking forward to having pictures and video of the day. I'm not envious of very many physical possessions, but I really do covet the photographs I see in my friends' homes. My best friend, Katie, has a side table in her living room that's covered in framed snapshots. Some of them are from milestone celebrations, like her high school graduation or her sister's wedding, but mostly they're candids taken on ordinary, happy days: in the pool with her niece in her floaties, or wearing a big smile and a jokey apron that matches her dad's at a Father's Day barbecue.

It breaks my heart to look at those photographs, because our family doesn't have a lot of them. There are tons of them from when I was a kid—in a bathing suit at the cabin by a lake in the woods where my parents used to take us, at my grandmother's house for Christmas, in my Girl Scout uniform. There are shots of me with my dad at Universal Studios, and me dressed to the nines with my mom before my cousin's wedding. There are pictures of me and my brother dressed up at Halloween, and ones from all the times as a little girl that I'd raid my mom's closet for makeup and heels.

And then they stop.

In a way, I'm not sorry—I don't think I could stand to

see the way I looked back when I was doing drugs, and I certainly wouldn't want to display a photograph of myself from that time. But it makes me sad that there aren't more pictures of me blowing out birthday candles or hugging my mom in front of my grandma's Christmas tree. It's also made me super-careful to document those happy occasions now; my family can hardly eat a regular weeknight dinner together without me jumping up to get a picture.

So I was devastated to learn that there wouldn't be any official pictures or video of one of the most important steps of my life. My mom had brought a camera, and she gave it to my dad so he could take pictures. Unfortunately, he didn't know how to use it. So there are no pictures at all, even amateur ones, of my baptism.

There we were by the side of that pool, freezing and unable to hear what the pastor was saying. I tried to concentrate on joy, on God's love, on what this day meant, but my nerves and physical discomfort were a constant distraction, as was my anxiety about what my father was thinking.

My mom went first so that she could be one of the attendants when it was my turn to be immersed. Honestly, at the time of my immersion, I didn't feel anything except the incredible, shocking coldness of the water. Afterward, I found myself standing by the side of the pool, shivering like a dog.

Then, right after it was over, my dad waved goodbye to

us and sped off. He'd been there, but he hadn't really been there. That feeling intensified when we were buttonholed by a man who'd seen his wife and daughter baptized that morning. His pride in his own family and the warmth of his congratulations for us stood in stark contrast to the way my own father had reacted. That stranger couldn't have been more lovely to us, but his excitement on our behalf did very little to lift my mood.

I was wet, freezing cold, and disappointed. My mom and I hustled inside to a bathroom to dry off and get warm, and as soon I was alone, I found myself fighting back tears. The whole event had been an incredible letdown.

I closed the door behind me and realized how scared I was. Then I started to pray. As I was detailing everything about the day that had been such a bitter disappointment, the enormity of what had taken place hit me. Of course it hadn't been easy or perfect, the way that I'd planned. What in my life had been? Coming to faith hadn't been easy or a perfect process, but I could clearly see that it was the best thing that I'd ever done. Forgiving my assailants hadn't been seamless either, but wrestling with that concept had been one of the most productive steps I'd taken toward moving my life forward. What good thing had ever been easy?

Maybe my father hadn't been effusive about my big day, but he'd shown up and supported us. And I had been baptized! I had been reborn into God's love. I was walking with Him now. And, meaningfully, my mother had been right by my side when I had been immersed. The idea that

I had been reborn in her arms, just as I had been placed into them after my physical birth, brought me to tears of awe and gratitude, replacing the self-pitying sniveling of a minute before.

I stood there in the bathroom, bathed in this feeling of complete gratitude. I had everything I needed. I had my faith, a God who knew me and loved me, who believed that I was perfect and who forgave me when I was not. I had a loving, supportive family—a mother who could join me in my faith and a dad who would support me even if he didn't entirely understand.

I didn't need pictures or a video, or a gloriously sunny Southern California day. I didn't need anything more than I had, which was a lot.

About a month after the ceremony, my baptism certificate arrived in the mail. When I looked at the date printed there, I felt a little ding of recognition in my head, but I couldn't say why. Later, I was having dinner at my parents' house. As I was helping my mom set the table, I asked her if she'd gotten her baptism certificate yet.

"It was weird," I told her. "When I opened mine, the date rang a bell. It seemed familiar to me, but I couldn't place it. February twenty-fourth. Is that someone's birthday or something?"

She looked at me and smiled. "No, but it should have been yours."

I was confused. "What do you mean? I was born January fifth."

"You were premature, remember? Your dad always says

you couldn't wait to get out, to take on the world." The enormity of what she was saying began to dawn on me, and the smile that crossed her face lit up the whole room. "That date was the first thing I noticed when I opened my own baptism certificate," she said. "February twenty-fourth was your original due date, Alisa."

After my baptism, there was a startling development in my relationship with my father: The tension eased up.

He'd been furiously grumpy, standing by the shallow pool for the ceremony. Afterward, he hadn't said a word to me about it. But I do think that seeing me take that step had been as transformative for him as it had been for me.

I think he'd come to understand why it had felt so important to me to make that commitment, and it had exposed him to the depth and intensity of my faith. It helped him to see that my decision wasn't personal or a betrayal of him or our family. I believe he finally understood what I'd been telling him all along, which was that I needed to get baptized for *me*.

My dad still has moments of conflict about my faith. The conversations between us are ongoing and can be difficult. But he can't deny the change in me since I've come to accept God in my life, and in many ways he's now very supportive. For example, my mom often gives me a wake-up call on Sunday mornings. (I do like my beauty sleep!) But these days, I'll hear my dad in the background: "Tell her to get her lazy butt out of that bed and into the shower, or she's going to be late for church." Things I thought I'd never hear!

There's been another surprising development in my relationship with my dad.

In the summer of 2013, I got laid off from the doctor's office where I'd been working as a medical assistant. It wasn't a huge surprise; we could all see that the practice couldn't support the number of staff we had working there, and I was the least senior employee. Everyone cried, including the doctor who delivered the news, but in some ways, it was a relief to me. I'd known for years that I didn't want to be in the medical field, even while I was putting myself through school.

Still, it was a scary summer. I have a lot of energy and still find myself prone to depression. Having the amount of free time you do when you're unemployed isn't a very good situation for me. School did keep me busy—I certainly couldn't complain anymore that I didn't have the time to do my best work, and my grades certainly benefited. But though I kept to a strict schedule of prayer and church, and I worked out a lot at the gym, there were still a lot of empty hours in the day.

I'm sure I don't need to tell anyone that it's a hard market for jobseekers out there. I applied for job after job after job, and went on interview after interview. Again I was reminded how important the years that I had lost had been. Instead of gaining relevant experience in the workforce, I'd been crawling from drug house to shady motel. Sure, I had experience as a meth dealer, but I couldn't put that on my resume.

Many of the applications asked if I'd ever been arrested, and I answered honestly, as I always do, even though I knew that in most cases, I wouldn't have the chance to explain the circumstances. Why would they care, anyway? I could easily see it from an employer's perspective: There were plenty of hungry, overqualified candidates out there without my erratic history.

It was a hard time for me. The good girl with the perfect grades had to deal with a lot of shame and guilt. I'd been at the top of my class. I was still someone who could spot a typo at twenty feet, someone who'd skip lunch and stay late to set up the kind of revolutionary filing system you didn't know enough to dream about. Now I couldn't get the most entry-level job out there, just so I could pay my bills? As the rejections piled up and my savings account ran low, I started to feel very scared.

Then I saw an ad for a receptionist at a Jewish temple. I applied. They called me in for an interview, and then another one. I had no idea that the position was to be the secretary for the rabbi until after they hired me.

I've been working at the temple for the past year and I can say without qualification that it's the best job I've ever had. I love interacting with the congregants, and I keep the bowl on my desk well-stocked with candy so they always have an excuse to stop by and chat. I love the rabbi and the executive director and all the other people I work with—especially how thoughtful and generous they are with their knowledge and time. I love how grateful my employers are when I go the extra mile. Mostly, I love working in a place of faith.

I wasn't sure when to tell everyone at the temple that I was a Christian, and I felt a little nervous about it. Technically, such a thing shouldn't matter, and everyone who interviewed me was careful not to ask. But when you're working in a religious environment, it's pretty much inevitable that the topic is eventually going to come up. I was delighted to find that there was no awkward weirdness at all—the opposite, in fact. That made me even happier to be working there.

The funny thing is that, working there, I've begun to learn a little bit about Judaism. I often call my dad with some tidbit or another that I've picked up over the course of the day. I've been particularly interested to learn how central the concept of forgiveness is in Judaism. So central, in fact, that the daily prayer that every Jew is supposed to say before bed, called the Shema, includes these lines: "Master of the Universe! I hereby forgive anyone who has angered or bothered me, or has sinned against me . . ."

The whole point of the Jewish high holiday called Yom Kippur—considered to be the holiest in the Jewish calendar—is forgiveness. You ask for forgiveness from God and other people, grant it to those who ask for it, and get closer to God because of this. I was astonished to learn that the faithful prepare for Yom Kippur by spending the ten days leading up to the holiday asking the forgiveness of everyone they feel they've harmed over the last year. (Hello, fourth step!) And when you are asked for forgiveness, you must grant it.

Of course, I'd love for my dad to become a Christian, to

be able to attend church with me and my mom every Sunday, and eventually to become baptized. But I plan to keep learning about Judaism and telling him what I've learned. I feel that any spiritual practice would make his life more meaningful and grant him some relief, which is what I want for my father—and what he deserves.

I go to church every Sunday with my mom. Our after-church park-and-chat routine has changed a little over the last year, but for a great reason: We've made some church friends. So, after my mom drives over to my house, we wait for our friends Stephanie and Lana to come over, and then we all drive to church together.

The four of us sit together and pray together. And then, after church, we all head over to a 1950s-themed diner I've been going to since I was a kid, where they push together a bunch of tables for us. My dad meets us there, along with my parents' oldest car-club friends, Pam and Mike. Lana's husband, Mike, comes, too, along with their grandson Daniel, who has started working for my dad.

The walls are lined with pictures of Marilyn Monroe and Elvis and the 1950s hotrods my parents and their friends love so much. Rosemary Clooney or Frank Sinatra is usually playing on the jukebox. I get the pumpkin pancakes if they have them—they are so good! The French toast combo with eggs and bacon is another favorite. The coffee is hot and delicious, and we love it when the owner comes over to shoot the breeze with us for a bit.

But the best part is seeing my dad at that table. We're not always talking about what happened at church, but the morning's sermon does come up from time to time. When it does, my dad's face doesn't close off the way it used to. He listens, and sometimes he argues. For me, the important part is that he's there and he's engaged. It means the world to me.

It might seem ironic that my baptism—the thing I thought would be the cause of so much chaos and conflict between my father and me—has turned out to be a source of a resolution instead.

*Trust in the Lord with all your heart, and do not lean on your own understanding.*

Then again, maybe the reconciliation that came about as a result of me getting baptized is just another example of why I follow God's will and not my own.

CHAPTER SIXTEEN

# *There Is an "After"*

One night, after speaking at an annual sexual assault awareness event, a woman approached me as I was packing up my things.

"I'm a victim, too," she said.

I looked up in alarm; her word choice had startled me deeply. In support training, we were careful to use the word *survivor*. The idea is that the word *victim* is passive—it robs the survivor of her agency and turns her into someone who was acted upon, whereas the word *survivor* highlights her resourcefulness and strength. It also acknowledges the strength required (often just to get through the day) in the aftermath of a trauma. Hearing the word *victim* when you're used to *survivor* can be jarring.

"It happened twenty-five years ago, but the rape still affects everything in my life," the woman, Carla, told me. "I still have nightmares, anxiety attacks. And forget about relationships. I can't even have friends. In fact,

I can barely have a conversation with the guy at the 7-Eleven."

That broke my heart. I took a closer look and realized that Carla's loneliness and hopelessness and lack of confidence were palpable. I asked her if she'd ever thought about seeing a therapist. "It helps to talk, to say what happened to us out loud," I told her.

But she immediately shut me down.

"Please. I'm in my fifties. There isn't anything that anyone can do for me now."

I realized then that her use of the word *victim* hadn't been accidental. *Victim* was the way she felt about herself. I felt myself getting upset. She reminded me of some of the older drug addicts I'd met when I was still using. "I'm not going to rehab," one longtime user had told me. "I don't need a crystal ball to know these drugs are what I'm going to die from."

Thinking about those drug addicts helped me to get past my momentary flash of upset and allowed me to feel hopeful on Carla's behalf. During the worst part of my drug use, I had also believed that I'd be an addict for the rest of my life. I'd truly thought the drugs would kill me, too. Still, I'd gotten clean, as bad off as I'd been. Maybe Carla could also get some help down the line and find some relief, see herself as a survivor rather than as a victim.

I wanted her to know that it's never too late; there's always an "after." I was living proof. It's hard to imagine a person much more in denial than I was the day Shirley took me down to Skid Row. And yet, as unbelievably resistant as I was, Shirley's efforts did plant a seed. God had watered that seed, tended it, and made it grow. So I looked at Carla, and thought: *Maybe I can plant a seed, too.*

Compassion flooded me, and I got up and gave her a hug.

"I can hear that it hurts," I told her. "But it doesn't have to feel this way. It's never too late to get help. And, Carla, see if it feels different to think of yourself not as a victim, but as a survivor."

On the drive home, I couldn't get Carla out of my head. I thought about my internal response when I'd heard Carla use the word *victim* to describe herself. It was then that I realized, with a little surprise, that I no longer considered myself to be a victim.

For a long time, I had parroted the party line that you hear in rape crisis centers: We're not victims; we're survivors. But although I was calling myself a survivor, I felt like a victim. I still blamed myself for what had happened. I still blamed my attackers for ruining my life. I was calling myself a survivor, but I was thinking—and acting— like a victim. But hearing Carla identify herself as a victim made me realize that, somewhere along the way, I'd begun to believe that I was a survivor. I'd been faking it until I felt it—but then I had felt it.

Sitting behind the wheel of my car, I couldn't help but wonder what had made the difference.

The answer I came up with was pretty simple: I'd made the transition from victim to survivor by finding meaning in what had happened to me.

\*     \*     \*

The Holocaust survivor and psychoanalyst Victor Frankl wrote a book called *Man's Search for Meaning*, which I found on the shelves in rehab. It's an incredible book; every trauma survivor should read it. Frankl believes that we can—and must—find meaning, even in the most extreme suffering. He says, "In some ways suffering ceases to be suffering at the moment it finds a meaning."

That is the lesson of Joseph's story, too. Like Victor Frankl's book, Joseph's story carries a lot of important messages for survivors.

First and foremost, his story speaks to me because it is a story about resilience. Over and over, Joseph endures truly horrible things, but he gets back up, stronger every time. He never allows his traumas, however significant and dreadful they may be, to determine his future. He doesn't dwell on them and allow them to hold him back. Instead, he determines his future. He fights for what he believes is his calling.

There is a very moving lesson here for me and for others who have survived trauma. We have to fight to learn what we are called to do, because doing that work is the best way to heal.

My calling, I believe—what God wants from me—is to help others who have suffered. It is to share what I now know—that there is an "after"—with Carla and other victims so that they can become survivors, too.

That's why the work I do with Project Sister is so

important to me. I want every girl I work with to understand that there is always cause for hope. For every one of us, there will be an "after."

I'm trying to spread that message elsewhere, too. Last year, a number of high-profile sexual assault cases were in the news. Many of them were reminiscent of my own case. Reading about them, I knew there was more that I could be doing to help. So, in the fall of 2013, I mustered my courage, sat down, and wrote a letter to the Jane Doe in the Steubenville rape case.

It took me a long time to write that letter. I must have written and rewritten it twenty-five times. I was scared that I would say the wrong thing to her, or that the very act of reaching out would be considered an intrusion. But I had the idea that this was my chance to write the letter I wished I could have received when I was in the worst parts of the aftermath of my own rape—during the abuse of the trials, after the hung jury. What did I wish someone would have said to me?

Once I thought about it that way, the words poured out of me onto the page. I told the Steubenville Jane Doe about my own story and the similarities I saw between her case and my own. Ultimately, I told her exactly what I wished someone had told me: that what happened wasn't her fault, no matter what anyone said. I told her that I was proud of her for seeking justice, and that there were thousands of people who believed and supported her. I told her what I now believe to be true (but something I would not have been able to hear at the time), which is that I hope she will eventually be able to find meaning in what had happened to her.

Mostly, I wanted to give her hope, because for me the hardest part was thinking that the anger and loneliness and shame that consumed me in the aftermath of my rape would be the way I felt forever.

"You have been through something that no one should ever have to endure," I wrote. "But I can promise the chaos, hurt, pain, and hopelessness *will not* last forever. There is a life for you beyond this; a beautiful life that is filled with happiness, hope, trust, and self-confidence."

In the very depths of my despair, I would never have been able to predict any of the wonders that the last four years have brought. Never! Who would have thought that I would get into college, let alone excel there? Who would have believed that my relationship with my parents would be closer now than it has ever been—even when I was little? That I would be on my way to forgiving my attackers, to letting go and being free of the anger and hate in my heart? That I would let my walls down and be open to relationships again, both new and old?

I certainly can't take the credit for any of these miracles. Indeed, the biggest surprise to the me of four years ago would have been that I live my life following God's will for me and not my own. I couldn't have predicted the close and beautiful relationship with God that I now enjoy, or the fact that I spend every day dedicated to living in Jesus's name and image. My faith has brought me a sense of peace, contentment, and security that I couldn't have imagined before.

If you'd shown me what the future held for me when I was sitting, humiliated, in a courtroom or smoking meth in a filthy squat, I would have told you that you were crazy. That's why I think it's so important to tell other survivors that there's an "after," and why I think it's even more powerful for them to hear it from me, someone else who didn't think there would be one.

I was very pleased to receive a short note back from the Steubenville Jane Doe. That first letter was hard to write, but I've written others since. There's plenty of evidence that she is a smart, strong girl with a lot of support. I follow all the cases in the news that seem similar to mine, and when it seems appropriate, I send a letter through the girl's lawyer. It's such a small thing, but it feels very healing for me to do. I can't know what it means to them to receive it, although the letters I've received in return are encouraging. But I know what it means to me to send them.

Part of the healing process is accepting your path: all of it, all of the things that happened to you, both the good and the bad. It will always be a temptation for me to see the rape as the incident that derailed my life. But the truth is that the trials God put in front of me have helped to build my character and my convictions. I have been tested—as so many of us will be. And I have survived, stronger for my tribulations.

There's another Victor Frankl quote that I keep on my wall: "The one thing you can't take away from me is the way I choose to respond to what you do to me. The last of one's freedoms is to choose one's attitude in any given circumstance."

Joseph exercises that choice. He could opt to see his years of imprisonment and servitude as the events that derailed his life. Instead, he says to his brothers, "God sent me ahead of you to preserve for you a remnant on earth and to save your lives by a great deliverance. So then, it was not you who sent me here, but God" (Genesis 45:7–8, NIV). Joseph chooses to see all the horrendous things that happened to him as an expression of God's will. He finds meaning in what happened to him instead of blame.

In this, and in all things, I try to emulate his example.

The men who assaulted me were released from prison at the beginning of 2008, after serving about three years each. That means the two trials together lasted longer than the time they spent in prison. This seems unjust to a lot of people, but, with Joseph and Dr. Frankl on my shoulder, I choose to see the outcome differently. First, I got more justice than a lot of victims do. According to RAINN, only 3 percent of rapists ever spend a day in prison—the other 97 percent of rapists go free. The aftershocks of my trials continued to be felt even after the sentences were served. It was the end of a corrupt era in Southern California government, and I choose to believe that it's an ending that came about because I didn't back down. I made a difference.

Today, I choose to find a tremendous amount of healing and meaning in the work that I do to support survivors. On the one hand, it would be very easy to get discouraged by how many sexual assault cases there are and how little

seems to change. Read the news, and it can seem depress-
ingly easy to rape a teenaged girl and get away with it. And
although they say that justice doesn't care about what's in
your wallet, I've noticed a disturbing trend: The men doing the raping tend to have more money and power than
the women they rape, and the more money and power those
guys and their families have, the more likely it is that the
charges will be dropped or reduced. Still, there's some evidence that there have been some positive changes on the
road to Jericho, and that's where I choose to dwell.

The work that matters to me most is the work I do with
survivors. I know there are a lot of people out there who are
struggling to find meaning in the terrible things that have
happened to them. Trust me: I know exactly how hard that
can be. And I know that I can't speak for them, or say how
they will find the meaning in their own trauma. Yet, I can
and will offer up one observation from my own life, in the
hope that it will help.

In Joseph's story, as in mine, there is a single alchemical
ingredient that transforms a series of horrific circumstances into a beautiful opportunity for grace. That ingredient is the same in Joseph's story as it is in my own: It is
forgiveness.

Martin Luther King Jr. once said that he was not going
to hate the white people of the South, because the burden
of hate was too much to bear. The burden of hate can be a
heavy one indeed, and I think Dr. King's example provides
very wise counsel for all of us who have been hurt and humiliated.

I would never say that I was thankful for what happened to me when I was sixteen. I don't believe that God wanted me to be abused with a lit cigarette; I don't think He wants that for anyone. But I can say that I am thankful for the changes that have taken place in me along the way. I am a different person than I would have been, that is for sure. And I know I am a better one.

# *Time to Grow*

When I started to write this book, I went up to my parents' attic to look through some of the boxes I'd stored there. I was looking for old journals, photo albums, or anything else I'd held onto that might jog my memory about what it felt to live through those times.

Those boxes provided quite a trip down memory lane. I found my perfect attendance certificates from junior high school, my Girl Scout sash with all my badges, ribbons from my cross-country track meets in freshman and sophomore years. I found some more upsetting things, too: my mom's calendar of our many legal appointments, as well as the meticulous notebooks in which she detailed the dates and times of all the harassment we endured.

And then, at the very bottom of the stack of boxes, I found one filled with what looked like shredded paper. My first glance at it confused me. What was this box of garbage, and why had I kept it?

Then I realized that it was the remains of the collage I'd ripped off the wall in my childhood bedroom. All the photographs of me with my high school friends, and all the inspirational quotes and words I'd spent hours pasting onto my wall were in that box.

My hands were shaking as I began to go through the scraps. Even so many years later, I could see why I'd been unable to sleep underneath it and why I'd ripped it down so viciously. Seeing the faces of those people, people who had hurt me both physically and emotionally, was like getting kicked in the gut.

But the thing that upset me most were the words and phrases I'd cut out of magazines, hoping that they'd inspire me in what I thought would be the next chapter of my life. Sifting through that box felt like I was sifting through the dreams I'd had for myself.

It took me a minute to regain my composure. I didn't think I was going to be able to go through it at all. But as I calmed down, I was struck by how many of those words and phrases still had relevance and resonance for me. I picked the tattered papers out of the box, one by one, making a makeshift collage on the ground at my feet.

*Fearless.*

When I saw that one, I nodded. I'd thought I'd known what fearlessness was when I'd pasted that to the wall, but I'd had no idea. Fear had fueled my desperate need to be popular in high school, at whatever cost; in retrospect, I could see that clearly. In the painful years after high school, too, there had been lot of occasions when my fear (and all the guilt and shame that went along with it) had almost completely consumed me.

That wasn't true anymore. I couldn't say, sitting in that attic, that I'd completely conquered fear, but it wasn't the driving engine of my life, as it had been for so long. I no longer looked to impress other people; the only being I cared about impressing was God.

The next fragment I picked out of that box was *Alive.*

That word gave me pause. Dying had only been an idea to me in high school. Doesn't every teenager think they'll live forever? I'd had no idea when I put that word on my wall how close I would come to losing my life—first on that pool table, and later with abusive men and the drugs I'd use to knock myself out. Even after I was clean and out of those abusive relationships, I'd spent another few years living a shadow life, circling around the emptiness at the center of my life. I'd been physically safe, maybe, but merely going through the motions. I couldn't really say I'd been alive.

Sitting back on my heels in the attic, I took a minute to thank God for my life—both for saving my life and for the fact that I hadn't died—and for helping me to find a sense of deep and important meaning, the kind that will animate and fill the rest of my days.

I reached back into the box.

*Light up.*

That phrase spoke to me, too. I remembered what I was thinking when I first glued it to the wall: I was dreaming about being the kind of girl whose brilliant sparkle and charisma can't help but catch every eye in the room. There were a lot of years of darkness after I'd put those words on my wall, years when I hadn't sparkled at all. But with God's help, I'd been able to throw open the curtains to let the light in. When it came, it wasn't the shallow, twinkly glitter I'd thought I wanted way back then, but a rich, warm, nourishing, energy-giving glow. And now it flooded every corner of my soul.

Again, I thanked God.

Then I came upon a phrase I hadn't remembered pasting on the wall at all: *Time to Grow.*

When I saw that one, all by myself in the attic, I laughed out loud.

*Time to Grow?* No kidding.

Sifting through the rest of the shreds of paper in that box, I felt a lot of tenderness for the hopeful young girl who'd knelt on her bed with a handful of magazine clippings and a glue stick. I was also able, at long last, to feel a lot of pride for the woman I've become. The words in the box were all the proof I needed that I hadn't lost the dreams I'd set out for myself. I was living them! True, I didn't find that dream where I thought I would, through the friends whose faces graced the wall next to those words, or through being popular, or by landing a big journalism job in New York. My path toward those dreams had not been the one I thought I would take. But neither could I have imagined how much more wonderful, how much more fulfilling and rich and deep, it would be to achieve them.

\*  \*  \*

My blessings surround me. I live about a mile and a half away from my parents, who stuck with me every step of the way and never stopped loving me. I have my own home, which is beautiful and safe. I have a good job, in a happy and supportive environment, and a place of faith. I am working toward my goal of becoming a victims' rights advocate at school. I'm grateful every single day for my good friends, for nature, and for my beautiful, sweet, loving dog.

I know that God blessed me with the ability to fight back and to prosecute my perpetrators. A lot of women don't have that because of shame, because they're afraid of retaliation, because nobody believes them, because there's no evidence. I take satisfaction in knowing that I testified and that my courage to do so resulted in imprisonment for the men who sexually assaulted me. I take satisfaction in the fact that they will have to register as sex offenders for the rest of their lives. In any case, I am happy to hand the ultimate responsibility for their justice over to God, while I work toward forgiving them.

I'm grateful, too, for the ability to tell my story. Whether I'm using it to help a young woman as I hold her hand in the emergency room, hours after her own sexual assault, or telling it to a room full of police officers so that they know a little better what to say and do when they're confronted with that woman, I'm blessed to be able to speak my truth, to see it resonate with people, and help them.

I won't lie. There are good days, and there are bad days, and sometimes the bad days are pretty bad. The bad days are the days I know that I need to dive deeper into my relationship with God, the days I have to pray even harder. I know He's always there, holding my hand, but on those days, I have to ask to feel Him.

And He always makes sure that I do.

# Acknowledgments

Where do I even begin when so many people have helped and supported me along my journey?

I must begin with God, because without Him and His redemption I would be nothing. Thank you, God, for always being my Savior, my life, my strength, my Redeemer, my grace, my forgiver, my freedom, my faith, my everything. I will always "wait on God."

To my other two biggest supporters, Mommy and Daddy: I cannot thank you both enough. Mommy, thank you for being my rock and keeping me strong. You have shown me what compassion and devotion truly are. Thank you for never letting me give up on God and for holding my hand until I was able to find Him and see that He had been holding my hand all along. Daddy, your heart is bigger than anybody's I will ever know, and it was you and your love that kept me alive and got me through the darkest times of my life. I'm blessed to be just like you, Daddy. Thank you, Mommy and Daddy, for never giving up on me even when I was ready to give up on myself. You both have taught me what unconditional love and support truly are. I love you both more than words could ever explain.

To my brother, Jaime: Thank you for not letting my past define the relationship that we have now. You are my big brother, and I will always look up to you. I love you.

To Grandma Kaplan: You have always believed in me and been by my side. I cannot thank you enough for the love and support you have always shown me, from being present at the trials and sentencing to being there to hear me speak at the march and rally. I love you with all my heart, Grandma.

And to Aunt Kathy: I owe my new life not only to God but also to you, because you were the one who knew the retreat was what I needed to change my life, and then Mommy made sure that I got there. Your dedication to helping me find God and a new life made all of this possible and allowed me to become the woman I am today. I will be forever grateful. I love you very, very much.

I would also like to send my deepest thanks and dearest regards to the following people.

Laura Tucker, thank you for all the long hours of listening to me babble on and on, and for being able to capture my voice in a way I never thought would be possible. This book would have never been a reality if it wasn't for you. I am forever grateful to you for the years you have dedicated your time, energy, passion, and commitment to this book. From the bottom of my heart, thank you.

Beka, you have remained the only true and constant friend in my life from the very beginning until now, and

I know that you will remain constant in my life until the very end. You have shown me what a true friend really is. You kept me from completely losing hope in friendships. I can't thank you enough. I love you.

Katie, thank you for all those nights that you reminded me that I am worth something and I am loved and lovable. You keep me focused on what is right and you understand me like no one else. Thank you for being my best friend. I love you, Boo.

Matt, thank you for the many times you listened and never judged me. Your continuous support over the years has been a blessing. Thank you for always being there with open arms and an open heart. I love you.

Shirley "GG," thank you for never giving up on me and fighting for me when I couldn't fight for myself. You are my pillar of strength, my inspiration, my mentor. Thank you for never letting me give up on myself and for always reminding me of my true self-worth. I'm blessed to have you be such a big part of my life. I love you with all my heart, GG.

Tiare, you have been my angel and my guiding light since the moment I met you in front of the hospital. Thank you for giving me peace and comfort during my most fearful times. It was that peace you showed me that helped inspire me to be the advocate I am today.

Susan Schroeder, thank you for fighting for me and for always doing what is right and never giving up. You are such a strong woman. I admire you and look up to you. I can't thank you enough for making this book happen because without you this would've never come to life. I love you.

# ACKNOWLEDGMENTS

Chuck Middleton, thank you for seeing me as a human being and not just another Jane Doe. Your passion, not only for me but for my case, is the reason we won. Your fight allowed me to get the justice I deserved. I will be forever grateful to you.

Tony Rackauckas, thank you for standing strong with me and all other women to make sure justice was done and time was served.

Scott Moxley, you stood up and fought for me in a way others were unable to. Your writing gave me a voice sometimes when I was unable to have one. I am eternally grateful for your unwavering support and belief in me.

Larry Welborn and Dave Lopez, thank you both for your continual support from the very beginning.

Brandi Bowles, thank you very much for all your time and commitment to me and this book. You put all the pieces together and made everything fall into place. Without your hard work this never could have happened. Thank you!

Jana Burson, your passion, enthusiasm, and drive for this project are the reasons it was able to come to light. I can't thank you enough for believing in me and my story.

JuLee Brand, thank you for making the cover come to life. Your vision was perfect and I am grateful "Grandpa Dean" was able to capture it. You are wonderful to work with, and I thank you for your commitment.

Jon Moonves, thank you for believing in me enough to help me get past my fears about writing a book. Without you guiding me through each step and getting me connected, this journey would have never taken place.

# ACKNOWLEDGMENTS

Laura Wheeler, Chelsea Apple, Louise Sommers, Shanon Stowe, and everyone else at Hachette and FaithWords who made this book possible, thank you from the bottom of my heart. Everyone's passion and dedication to my story were more than I could have ever asked for. Thank you for making what was once only a dream a reality.

To all others who have helped me and supported me along my journey, my heart is forever filled with gratefulness and love for you all. Thank you always.

# Resources

If you have been sexually assaulted, please know that you are not alone, and that help is available.

**RAINN (RAPE, ABUSE AND INCEST NATIONAL NETWORK)**
1220 L Street, NW
Suite 505
Washington, DC 20005
202-544-3064
RAINN.org

RAINN is the country's largest anti–sexual violence organization. Their website is rich with resources and information on surviving sexual assault.

**NATIONAL SEXUAL ASSAULT HOTLINE**
800-656-HOPE (4673)
https://ohl.rainn.org/online

This confidential hotline is run by RAINN. Although it's a national hotline, the person at the other end works at a rape crisis center in your area and can give you information about counseling, community resources, and a variety of other questions. Because the calls are answered locally, the information you'll get will be tailored to the laws and protocol in your state.

## THE JOYFUL HEART FOUNDATION
212-475-2026 (New York); 808-531-3520 (Honolulu)
joyfulheartfoundation.org

The actor Mariska Hargitay (*Law and Order: SVU*) runs a foundation with a number of amazing resources. Her vision is of "a community with no sexual assault, domestic violence and child abuse." The foundation's mission is "to heal, educate and empower survivors of sexual assault, domestic violence and child abuse, and to shed light into the darkness that surrounds these issues."

The foundation provides resources for survivors as well as their caretakers and educators.